Business Leaders and Leadership in Asia

The quality of its business leadership is a key issue for the future development of Asia's economies. Although Asia's economies have grown spectacularly in recent decades, they are currently facing increasing challenges. This book explores the current state of business leaders and leadership in Asia. It demonstrates that there is no single model of Asian business leadership, and that Western models often do not fit easily alongside Asian cultural values. It discusses how relatively developed Asian economies – Japan, Korea, Taiwan and Singapore, and former socialist economies – China and Vietnam – all have different types of business leadership challenges at present. The book concludes by assessing how business leadership in Asia is likely to develop in the future.

Ying Zhu is Professor and Director of the Australian Centre for Asian Business, University of South Australia.

Shuang Ren is a Senior Lecturer in the Deakin Business School, Deakin University, Australia.

Ngan Collins in a Senior Lecturer in the Business College, RMIT University, Australia.

Malcolm Warner is an Emeritus Professor and Fellow of Wolfson College and the Judge Business School, University of Cambridge, United Kingdom.

Routledge Studies in the Growth Economies of Asia

Business Leaders and Leadership in Asia

Ying Zhu, Shuang Ren, Ngan Collins and Malcolm Warner

LONDON AND NEW YORK

First published 2018
by Routledge

2 Park Square, Milton Park, Abingdon, Oxfordshire OX14 4RN
52 Vanderbilt Avenue, New York, NY 10017

Routledge is an imprint of the Taylor & Francis Group, an informa business

First issued in paperback 2019

Copyright © 2018 Ying Zhu, Shuang Ren, Ngan Collins and Malcolm Warner

The right of Ying Zhu, Shuang Ren, Ngan Collins and Malcolm Warner to
be identified as authors of this work has been asserted by them in
accordance with sections 77 and 78 of the Copyright, Designs and Patents
Act 1988.

All rights reserved. No part of this book may be reprinted or reproduced or
utilised in any form or by any electronic, mechanical, or other means, now
known or hereafter invented, including photocopying and recording, or in
any information storage or retrieval system, without permission in writing
from the publishers.

Notice:
Product or corporate names may be trademarks or registered trademarks,
and are used only for identification and explanation without intent to
infringe.

British Library Cataloguing in Publication Data
A catalogue record for this book is available from the British Library

Library of Congress Cataloging in Publication Data
A catalog record for this book has been requested

ISBN: 978-1-138-83136-0 (hbk)
ISBN: 978-0-367-87128-4 (pbk)

Typeset in Times New Roman
by Taylor & Francis Books

Contents

Tables

1 Introduction

Challenges of business leaders and leadership in Asia

Introduction

Asia has become the centre of global attention. Amidst the debt that has been plaguing the US and Europe since the 2008 financial crisis, rapid growth in most parts of Asia, in particular Southeast Asia, provides promising business opportunities for new global expansion. The combined effects of strong market potential, rapid foreign direct investment (FDI) intake and unprecedented openness to the external world evident in Asian countries have generated increasing attention worldwide. The effects of Asia's growth are so significant that, in 2012, the US Government declared its Asia Pivot strategy with a shift of focus to this region. Around the same year the Australian Government released its *Australia in the Asian Century* White Paper (Australia Government, 2012), projecting the scale and scope of Asia's rise by 2025.

Navigating the fast-growing Asian region is nonetheless never an easy journey, despite the potential for global business. No single model exits to provide guidelines on how to do business and manage a workforce effectively in Asia. The region is the world's largest and most culturally diverse area, and is characterized by uneven development in economic, social, political and cultural realms. This heterogeneity applies as much to contextual contingencies at various levels (e.g. state, industry and organization) as to managerial cognition and action. The implicit expectations of how a business leader looks and behaves are not always consistent with stereotypical Western leader-like traits and behaviours. The complexity is further exacerbated by the expansion of Western-derived best practices and management philosophies which often encounter resistance or challenges from indigenous ways of thinking and acting. What is considered logical and rational judgement in Western approaches is not necessarily perceived in the same way in Asia. Therefore, it is timely to carry out this research on analysing business leaders and leadership in the Asian region so that both Asian people and others have a better understanding of the characteristics of their respective leadership concepts and practices in comparison with others. This is the rationale that underpins this book.

Setting out a model

This book sets out to explore the sense and sensibility surrounding the perceptions and practices of business leaders, leadership and management in Asia, based on a cross-country comparative approach. Given that the challenges and opportunities encountered in the landscape of business operation are heterogeneous in nature, the analysis in this book encompasses two major groups of Asian countries and regions. The first group includes advanced economies (i.e. Japan, South Korea, Taiwan and Singapore) that have enjoyed better established economic structure, institutional framework and more experience of dealing with global issues. The challenges they face are staggering economies and the struggle to sustain growth amidst fierce competition from neighbouring countries and Western economies. The second group includes socialist market economies (i.e. China and Vietnam) where many emerging issues and uncertainties provide new thinking and new ways of developing capable leaders. As previously state-controlled communist regimes, these two countries are undertaking ongoing economic reforms and opening-up that are anchored in rapid restructuring and changes in formal and informal institutions. Compared to their neighbours in the first group, China and Vietnam face challenges such as a lack of rule of law, infrastructure and know-how, thereby presenting more difficulties for business leadership. This group provides insights into how business leaders can survive in such a harsh environment, and presents a rich context in which to examine business leadership.

Challenging issues

This book first asks and seeks to address challenging issues such as what constitutes effective leader behaviours in the exemplar Asian countries. We position our exploration within a unique context characterized by paradoxes (Warner, 2014). The six case study economies belong to the Confucian Asian Clusters in which the management and leadership theory and practices are shaped by Confucian values (Chhokar et al., 2012). In fact, Confucianism is so woven into the fabric of these societies that terms such as 'Confucian Management', 'Confucian Capitalism' and 'Confucian HRM' have been coined to describe the philosophical roots of their business management, an intellectual attempt that is rare in the Western literature (Warner, 2014; Warner, 2017). The enhanced trans-national interactions facilitated by globalization raise a question as to what extent traditional thinking in general, and Confucianism in particular, is still relevant to differentiate effective business leaders; relatedly, to what extent the exogenous (i.e. Western) management influences, such as the US-derived leadership concepts (see Warner, 2016), shape the criteria people use to evaluate the effectiveness of business leaders, formally or implicitly.

Tension is therefore a recurring theme in this book when we discuss the specificities of each country. A common tension faced by our case study countries and regions is the dynamic interplay between indigenous management/ leadership practices and influences such as Confucian values and imported ones from the West. As one author has commented: 'Such exogenous ideas … were to blend with indigenous ones. They were diffused, then adapted, and finally absorbed into local practices, where deemed appropriate' (Warner, 2016, p. 619).

The manifestation of this interplay takes many specific forms. As Zhu observes in Chapter 3, Japanese businesses and leaders resorted to the traditional 'tinkerer' spirit as a solution to domestic challenges in recognition of the limitations associated with the adoption of Western management theories and practices. Ren makes the comment in Chapter 6 that the Chinese government reintroduced Confucian values in an attempt to build national identity and facilitate a healthy business and societal environment.

Fundamentally, the variations of how businesses and business leaders cope with paradoxical demands are rooted in the stages of the economic and societal development of these countries and regions. As Child (2009, p. 58) explains:

> to the extent that societies pass through similar stages of development, this cautions against assuming that every country's context is unique because apparent contemporary differences may become similarities when viewed historically.

The historical, cultural and social embeddedness of this book therefore sets it apart from prior management and leadership studies that take mainly a psychological approach to depicting leader traits, characteristics and personality (see Yukl, 2012). A fine-grained understanding of leadership vis-à-vis contexts also provides direction for a comparison and synergy of effective leader behaviours across different countries.

In addition, we seek to address the challenge of developing sustainable leadership competencies for the future. We started the analysis by exploring the key leadership qualities that are most in need of development. Indeed, top business leaders and managers at all levels are under pressure to deal with unprecedented challenges in a global context, making global mindsets and cross-cultural capabilities pivotal to their survival and success. The complexity of these challenges facing business leadership in Asia requires continuous updating of knowledge and skills through a variety of means, including self-development and institutionalized training. Whenever possible, we substantiate our analysis with a brief description of exemplar business leaders who act as role models or sources of inspiration for leader development in their respective countries.

Structure of the book

This book is organized according to three broad sections. This introductory chapter sets the scene and is followed by Chapter 2, which provides a systematic theoretical and background overview pertinent to business leaders and leadership in general. The purpose of the second chapter is to establish the theoretical foundation which helps readers trace the current leadership perceptions and practices to their cultural and institutional roots. The embedded nature of leadership is further instantiated in Chapters 3–8, which present country-specific profiles detailing traditional normative values on leadership, influences of Western management practices, tensions and concerns of current business leaders, leader development, and providing an evaluation and conclusion. These chapters are based upon our recent fieldwork with business leaders and scholars in the respective economies, coupled with our research experiences in the relevant literature. The book is concluded in Chapter 9, which provides a comparative analysis of East Asian economies, as well as a comparison between East and West. The value of this book lies in offering path-dependent possibilities of leadership and an integrated framework to analyse, compare and contrast Asian countries within the spheres of regional disparity.

Conclusion

Influenced by globalization, business leadership competencies nowadays are in flux as never before. The changing leadership competencies reflect dynamism within a particular society, encompassing its economic, political, legal and other institutional characteristics. The dynamic institutional context makes the legitimacy of business operation an emerging challenge in Asian countries. In undertaking this work, our book has focused on leadership challenges, in particular related to sense and sensibility of managerial cognition and action. Sense and sensibility highlight the tensions between professional and logical judgement influenced by Western-derived practice and culture and following one's heart and passion based on innate and ingenious values. Correspondingly, the book examines the different ways business leaders improve their leadership competencies to navigate their complex and dynamic environments. For this reason, this book is suitable for scholars and practising consultants who are interested in understanding how and why business leadership is currently perceived and practised in Asia, and how to manage the workforce in domestic companies as well as multinational corporations (MNCs) in the region.

References

Australia Government (2012) 'Australia in the Asian Century,' White Paper, http://asia ncentury.dpmc.gov.au/white-paper [accessed on 15 November 2016].
Chhokar, J. S., Felix, C. B. and House, R. J. (eds) (2012) *Culture and Leadership across the World: The GLOBE Book of In-Depth Studies of 25 Societies*, London and New York: Routledge.
Child, J. (2009) 'Context, comparison, and methodology in Chinese management research', *Management and Organization Review*, 5(1): 57–73.

Warner, M. (2014) *Understanding Management in China: Past, Present and Future*, London and New York: Routledge.

Warner, M. (2016) 'Whither "Confucian Management?"', *Frontiers of Philosophy in China*, 11(4): 608–632.

Warner, M. (ed.) (2017) *The Diffusion of Western Economic Ideas in East Asia*. London and New York: Routledge.

Yukl, G. (2012) 'Effective leadership behavior: What we know and what questions need more attention', *Academy of Management Perspective*, 26(4): 66–85.

2 Business leaders and leadership in Asia

Underpinning theories and background

Introduction

Business leaders and leadership in Asia give rise to complex and profound issues, given the wide range of influences of philosophical, historical, cultural, social, political and economic factors, as well as management/leadership theories and practices, from the East and the West. In order to clarify such complex issues and reach a better understanding of the underpinning theories and contextual factors, this chapter aims to illustrate the relevant theoretical thinking of East and West regarding leaders and leadership, comparing and contrasting common elements as well as differences. In doing so, we can set up a solid platform for the case studies presented in the chapters that follow, in order to discuss and debate the key themes accordingly. These chapters will enable us to identify the key findings and major contributions of this book in the concluding chapter.

In order to elaborate these key issues, this chapter is designed with the following structure: following the introductory section, the chapter focuses on the identification of key aspects in mainstream Western leadership literature from the perspective of a historical evolution process. A number of these Western approaches have also been introduced and adopted in East Asian countries, with modification and combination with the respective Eastern philosophical thinking and practices. An illustration of Eastern thinking and practices regarding leaders and leadership is then presented with a discussion on how these have influenced current business leaders and leadership in East Asia. In the final section, we compare and contrast similarities and differences between Eastern and Western thinking and practices regarding leaders and leadership, and develop a number of key questions for consideration in the relevant arguments in the chapters to come.

The key aspects of Western leadership literature

As in most social science studies, the study of leadership reflects the broad trends in deep thinking, with evidence of contextual factors (Lord et al., 2016). The evolution of research on leadership in the early years placed emphasis on the social, psychological and functional/task (management) contexts influencing the leadership process. Followers' performance, for instance, affected their supervisor's leadership style (Lowin and Craig, 1968); situational factors were more important than individual differences in leader decision-making styles (Hill and Schmitt, 1977); leader behaviour changed substantially as a function of task (Hill and Hughes, 1974); and outcomes of leadership style also depended on the leadership situation (Fiedler, 1964). Based on these early years of leadership studies, a key aspect emerged indicating that leadership style was a flexible, social and task-dependent process (Lord et al., 2016).

In addition, early research focused on stable aspects of leaders, such as traits or styles, as primary determinants of leadership (Lord et al., 2016). Hence, leadership was viewed mainly in terms of entity rather than process, and most of the early research conceptualized differences among leaders in terms of behavioural styles. The perceived leadership styles as reported by a leader's followers were being seen as valid measures of leader behaviour. However, what was missing was the consideration that followers integrate their perceptions of leadership with other aspects of situation, such as group performance, liking of the leader, follower affective states and task knowledge. These factors also influence ratings of leadership (Keller Hansbrough et al., 2015). Therefore, there was a need to develop a deeper level of understanding and measurement of leadership perceptions, leading to the emergence of social cognitive approaches to the study of leadership (Lord et al., 2016).

The social cognitive approaches to leadership showed that for both leaders and followers, interpretation of leadership processes and outcomes was a critical mediating process linking leaders and followers (Martinko and Gardner, 1987). In order to identify and categorize leadership, a central category prototype was developed to help perceivers understand leadership, defined as either transactional or transformational leadership in early years, and later as charismatic, situational, servant, ethical and others (i.e. later development of authentic, transpersonal, sustainable leaderships and so on) which we will elaborate more in the later part of this chapter. In this sense, categorization theory provided a natural linkage to trait theories of leadership, such as a strong relationship between the intelligence of a leader and leadership perceptions (Lord et al., 1986).

In the late 1970s and 1980s, a new approach, namely attribution theory, emerged which looked at leaders' attributional processes as antecedents to their responses to subordinate performance (Green and Mitchell, 1979). Two important conclusions were made through this approach: 1) how supervisors responded to subordinate performance was mediated by their sense-making process; and 2) both supervisors and subordinates adjusted their behaviour to situational factors as they understood them (Matinko and Gardner, 1987). However, Lord et al. (2016) claimed that social cognitive theory with systematic and thoughtful attributional process was the exception rather than the rule because people make sense using automatic processes, influenced by their culture, personal traits and even emotional states (Naidoo and Lord, 2008). However, we cannot deny the richness of understanding of the factors affecting leadership perceptions and processes which reflect the cumulative advance in social cognitive approaches to leadership.

Another prominent theme in leadership theory is based on the social exchanges among leaders and followers, indicating a closer tie to Eastern philosophy and behaviour. One typical example is the Vertical Dyad Linkage (VDL) approach, which views the particular relationships between a leader and each follower as the basic unit of analysis and as their unique social exchange relationship (Dansereau et al., 1973). The social exchanges and roles are negotiated over time, and depend on both supervisor and subordinate (Graen and Uhl-Bien, 1995). This approach was extended to the social network perspective, with the emphasis on multiple ties among employees and an expanding social context of the VDL.

In more recent years, the relationship-based approach to leadership has been extended as Leader–Member Exchange (LMX) theory, which emphasizes team-member exchange as well as organizational context (Seers, 1989). The LMX theory has two focuses, one on antecedents and the other on outcomes. One antecedent is the regulatory focus of followers with the activation of ideal vs. ought identities. It suggests that ultimately it is identities that underlie the nature of effective leader–member exchanges (Jason and Johnson, 2012). Hence, a subordinate's identification (relational identification) with the subordinate–manager role relationship can be the basis for organizational identification, and this reflects the appropriate activation of identities and motivational processes as a guide to role-making as well as the more diffuse cognitive, affective and behavioural processes (Lord et al., 2016). With regard to identifying outcomes, a number of items can be included, such as satisfaction with working relationships, in-role and extra-role performance, citizenship behaviour, and turnover intention and actual turnover (Lord at al., 2016).

Based on both social cognitive and social exchange literatures, a new approach of self-concept/identity emerged in the late 1990s and 2000s. One core notion of this approach was that these mental constructs and their social manifestation create a 'force for action' (Oyserman et al., 2012). One's origins in the past, interpretation of the present, and projection into the future depend on 'identity work' (Ibarra and Barbulescu, 2010). The individual active identity becomes a mediating structure linking contextualized interpretation to situationally appropriate behaviour (Bargh et al., 2008). One important element of self-concept is self-schemas being derived from past experience and presented in verbal, visual, and embodied forms (Markus and Wurf,1987) with consistent beliefs about one's qualities or one's behaviour in a given domain, such as 'being a leader' (Kunda, 1999). With regard to a leader in a working situation, the Working Self-Concept (WSC) was identified as a set of active self-schemas (Markus and Wurf, 1987), and active WSCs automatically guide a leader's judgement, behaviour, self-regulation and social perceptions.

Hence, active self-schemas can become conscious, and foster the creation of a consistent schema, but situationally integrated identity (Dehaene, 2014). Such an integrated identity can be found at three different levels, including: 'individual self' with one's distinctiveness from others in terms of traits or abilities; 'relational self' with one's (leader) role relationship with others; and 'collective self' with one's (leader) group membership and self-worth within the group. In other words, such self-constructs can integrate self-concepts at levels of 'who I am', 'who we are' or 'how our group compares to others' (Sluss and Ashforth, 2008; Sluss et al., 2012). In addition, self-concepts of followers can also be influenced by leaders, creating powerful and multi-dimensional effects on the way followers construct their own identities, determining behaviours, attitudes and evaluative structures (Lord and Brown, 2004). As for effective leadership, by influencing active identities at appropriate levels, leaders can create a cascade that affects the meaning of a task for an individual, the goal set by that individual and the way information is processed (Dragoni, 2005).

Hence, recent research, with its focus on identity as an important construct in leadership development, draws the links between the development of leader identity and leadership effectiveness (Day and Sin, 2011). The concept of self with multilevel identities has also helped combine individual self with relational and collective orientation. This new approach to self-concept may bring Western concepts of individualism much closer to the Eastern concept of relationship and collectivism.

The evolution of research on leadership indicates that research in the early years emphasized the important effects of social, psychological and functional/ task (management) contexts on the leadership process. However, some fundamental questions – namely, why is leadership needed at all, who emerges as a leader, and how can a leader be effective? – have not been asked and challenged (Zehnder et al., 2017). As parallel research to the literature on management and psychology, leadership in economics has developed to argue these fundamental issues. Within this context, it is seen that market exchanges lead to an excessive search for cost bargaining and generate the potential for exploitation, undermine investment incentives, limit cooperation or trigger free-riding. Hence, effective leaders can use their formal authority not only to diminish inefficiencies caused by searching, haggling and opportunistic behaviour, but they can also foster coordination and cooperation within their workforce. Therefore, transaction cost economics calls for a richer role of leadership because markets fail to implement efficient team production. In addition, careful leader selection and institutional safeguards are of crucial importance in order to avoid imminent danger that a leader abuses the power for opportunistic reasons (Zehnder et al., 2017).

So far, research on leader emergence has mostly focused on the psychological traits of the individuals who emerge as leaders (i.e. trait theory), and why these individuals are naturally followed by others (i.e. social cognitive theory). However, from an economic point of view, effective leadership requires: 1) the right leader to be selected with the necessary decision-making power; and 2) the selected leader to apply the leadership strategy best suited to the situation (i.e. situational leadership). Hence, leadership research should focus on the interplay between the situation and the person (Zehnder et al., 2017). For example, an organization's ownership structure as a particular situation influences the decision-making power and control rights of leaders, and effective leadership requires the necessary degree of control over decisions within the organization. The crucial issue related to effective leadership is that effective leaders are able to develop strategies to lead according to a particular situation (i.e. situational) based on their own capabilities and experiences (i.e. trait).

More critical views on individual prototypes of leadership style have also been developed in recent years. For example, literature on the principal-agent concept points out that although transactional leadership tools such as monetary incentives and direct control can have substantial positive effects on follower motivation in simple environments, there is a danger of incentives with unwanted or distortive implications in more complex environments (Zehnder et al., 2017). In addition, research on transformational leadership as well as related approaches such as charismatic, visionary and inspirational leadership suggests that the effective leaders can go beyond transactional measures. Effective leaders can shape their followers' behaviour through their personal abilities to persuade and motivate. For example, transformational leaders inspire their followers by providing them with a common mission and vision, and by giving them a sense of identity, turning outsiders into insiders within the organization and incorporating their common goals.

A charismatic leadership approach can also influence followers' behaviours whereby leaders become 'meaning makers' with the ability to provide a compelling vision for followers along Weberian lines. The amount of charisma attributed to a leader increases as the leader's vision becomes more idealized in the minds of followers (Khatri et al., 2001). Based on this approach, an ideal leader is visionary, practical and inspirational, and serves followers well (i.e. servant leadership) with inspiration and moral example (Graham, 1991).

Based on these considerations, authentic leadership approaches emerge by incorporating the abovementioned approaches – including transformational, charismatic, servant, inspirational, ethical and moral approaches – along with other forms of positive leadership (Banks et al., 2016). According to Walumbwa et al. (2008), authentic leaders are described as being self-aware, showing openness and clarity regarding who they are, and consistently disclosing and acting in accordance with their personal values, beliefs, motives and sentiments. In other words, there are four components of authentic leadership, namely self-awareness, relational transparency, balanced processing and an internalized moral perspective (Banks et al., 2016). From a social information processing perspective, research shows that authentic leaders and followers who share cooperative goals related to developing a climate for inclusion can prompt the vicarious learning of inclusive behaviours by followers, facilitating goal attainment for both parties (Boekhorst, 2014). Adding further value, a more recent approach based on transpersonal leadership has emerged with the concept of leaders operating beyond their own egos while continuing personal development and learning (Coyne, 2017). These leaders are radical, ethical and authentic, as well as emotionally intelligent and caring. They are able to embed authentic, ethical and emotionally intelligent behaviours into the DNA of the organization, to build strong collaborative relationships, and to create a performance-enhancing culture that is ethical, caring and sustainable. In order to achieve sustainable leadership, leaders must be happy, healthy and therefore sustainably high performing (Coyne, 2017).

A study of the evolution of leadership research development hence indicates that recent research on leadership tends to move towards more integrative approaches such as inclusive, plural, collective, cooperative, relational, social networks, shared and interdependent elements, with an emphasis on balance and long-term sustainability (see Carter et al., 2015; Chrobot-Mason et al., 2016; Rockstuhl et al., 2012). This trend indicates a departure from the conventional Western individualistic and short-term approaches towards a more balanced (i.e. based on *Yin* and *Yang*), collective and relational-based thinking which appears to come closer to Eastern philosophical thinking and practices. Our focus will shift to these issues in the following section.

Underpinning philosophical thinking and practices of leadership in East Asia

The foundation of East Asian philosophical thinking can be traced back to the ancient Chinese traditional philosophies – the most prominent being Confucianism, Daoism, *Yi Jing* (the Book of Changes), *Bing fa* (War Strategy), Legalism and Mohism during the 'Spring–Autumn and Warring-States' period (771–221 BC) – as well as other religious influences such as Buddhism in the later years. In this chapter, we focus on philosophical elements that bear directly on leadership practices in East Asia.

The most influential traditional philosophy in China and other East Asian countries such as Japan, Korea, Singapore, Taiwan and Vietnam is Confucianism. Confucius (Kongzi, 551–479 BC) developed a set of teachings based on absolute respect for tradition (early Zhou Dynasty) and on a carefully ranked hierarchy founded on primary relationships between members of families and between the people and their rulers (De Mente, 1994). It has been seen as a philosophy guiding people's daily life. The major ideas of Confucius were based on: three fundamental guiding figures (i.e. ruler guides subject, father guides son and husband guides wife); five constant virtues (i.e. benevolence, righteousness, propriety, wisdom and fidelity); and the doctrine of the mean as *zhong yong* (i.e. midway or harmony). Confucius believed that *Ren*, or human heartedness/benevolence, is the highest virtue an individual can attain, and this is the ultimate goal of education (McGreal, 1995). *Ren* is a strictly natural and humanistic love, based upon spontaneous feelings cultivated through education. It advocates love for all people and doing good for the populace, as depicted in the ethos 'troubled, improve yourself; valued, improve the world'. Benevolence requires a leader to be caring, to respect his people and to set a good example, so that followers accept their place in the social hierarchy, engage in cooperative human harmony and have confidence in their leader (see Warner, 2016). Although such ideas appear to resemble elements of contemporary transformational leadership, Confucianism does not perceive leaders as agents of change, as transformational leadership theorists do (see Rindova and Starbuck, 1997). Moreover, Confucianism combines charisma and morality by maintaining that human nature is inherently good and that people can be swayed by the power of words.

In turn, the path to the attainment of *Ren* is the practice of *Li*, which represents social norms. *Li* can be interpreted as rituals, rites or proprieties. In its broadest sense, the term includes all moral codes and social institutions. In its fundamental but narrow sense, it means socially acceptable forms of behaviour (McGreal, 1995). In addition, *Li* involves the deliberate devices used by the sages to educate people and maintain social order.

Since *Li* is a term for moral codes and social institutions, people are tempted to think that the practice of *Li* is to enforce conformity with social norms at the cost of individuality (McGreal, 1995). However, in Confucianism, an individual is not an isolated entity. Confucius said, 'In order to establish oneself, one has to establish others. This is the way of a person of *Ren*' (McGreal, 1995: 5). Therefore, individualization and socialization are but two aspects of the same process.

The principle governing the adoption of *Li* is *Yi*, which means righteousness or proper character, and is a principle of rationality. *Yi* is the habitual practice of expressing one's cultivated feeling at the right times and in the right places. Confucius said: '*Junzi* (a perfect person or superior) is conscious of, and receptive to *Yi*, but *Xiaoren* (a petty person) is conscious of, and receptive to gains' (McGreal, 1995: 6).

According to Confucius, the right method of governing is not by legislation and law enforcement, but by supervising the moral education of the people (McGreal, 1995: 6). The ideal government for him is a government of *wuwei* (non-action), as with the Daoists, through the solid groundwork of moral education, said to be a precursor of the later notion of *laissez-faire*. The reason given by Confucius is:

> If you lead the people with political force and restrict them with law and punishment, they can just avoid law violation, but will have no sense of honour and shame. If you lead them with morality and guide them with *Li*, they will develop a sense of honour and shame, and will do good of their own accord.
>
> (McGreal, 1995: 7)

This is the doctrine of appealing to the human heart: self-realization toward world peace (harmony) and a peaceful world and orderly society are the ultimate goals of Confucianism.

Confucianism dominated Chinese philosophy for many years. However, other philosophies before and after Confucius were also influential, albeit with different focuses. Daoism is another influential thinking school. The founding father of Daoism, Lao Zi (6th century BC?), introduced the idea of yielding to the primordial ways of the universe (Whiteley et al., 2000). Everything in the universe follows certain patterns and processes that escape precise definition and, imprecisely, this is called *Dao*, the 'Way' (McGreal, 1995: 9). In his work entitled *Daode Jing* (Classic of the Way and Its Power), Lao Zi claimed that *De* (virtue) cannot be strived for, but emerges naturally. The best 'Way' to act or think is *wuwei* (effortless activity).

However, the most important element of Daoism is 'oneness' and *Yin–Yang*. Lao Zi indicated that *Dao* produces one. One produces two. Two produces three and three produces 10,000 things (i.e. everything). The 10,000 things carry *Yin* and embrace *Yang*. By combining these forces, harmony is created (Daode Jing, Verse 42). These can be understood as the fundamentals of the universe, which contains the polar complements of *Yin* and *Yang*: while *Yin* represents the dark, recessive, soft, feminine, low, contractive, centripetal, short, hollow, empty, and so forth, *Yang* represents the bright, dominant, hard, masculine, high, expansive, centrifugal, long, full, solid, and so forth. Nothing is ever purely one or the other; rather, all things are in flux between one pole and its opposite (McGreal, 1995: 14).

In addition, *De* is the second important concept within Daoism. *De* (usually translated as 'virtue' or 'power') is a thing's personal stock of *Dao*, or, put another way, it is the natural potential or potency instilled within one. In contrast to Confucius, who referred to *De* as a moral term, for Lao Zi, *De* signified natural abilities that enable things to be their best spontaneously and effortlessly (McGreal, 1995: 13). Furthermore, Lao Zi argued that once ineffectual *Ren* has degenerated into rules, the conditions for conflict, rebellion and repression have emerged. Since rules advise doing something unnatural, there will always be someone who will refuse to comply. For a rule to remain meaningful and not become an empty rule, compliance must be enforced (McGreal, 1995: 13).

For Lao Zi, balance between the poles does not mean static parity, but a dynamic reversion that perpetually counterbalances all propensities toward one extreme or the other. However, the world tends to privilege the *Yang* while ignoring or denigrating the *Yin*. Daoism aims to re-balance things by emphasizing *Yin* over *Yang*. In *Daode Jin*, Lao Zi claimed:

> Human beings are born soft and flexible; when they die they are hard and stiff. Plants arise soft and delicate, when they die they are withered and dry. Thus, the hard and stiff are disciples of death; the soft and flexible

are disciples of life. An inflexible army is not victorious; an unbending tree will break.

(Daode Jing, Verse 76)

Therefore, Daoism provides enlightenment for human beings to understand and follow the fundamental cycle of the universe.

Dao is the essence of Oneness and the *Yi Jing* (The Book of Changes) is the everchangingness of that Oneness (Chu, 1995). According to tradition, the book was composed in several layers over many centuries, and it was initially a manual of divination; but with the 'Ten Wings' appendices attached, the resultant *Yi Jing* may be considered a work of philosophy. McGreal (1995: 60) claims that the Book of Changes has provided the stimulus for some of the most creative and useful thinking by Chinese seers and scholars. In both its naive and its sophisticated uses the book has intrigued the Chinese mind and definitively affected the Chinese concept of the cosmos and of the relations of human beings to the continuing changes that are the foreseeable outcome of the universal interplay of opposing natural forces.

As these thoughts were debated in the intellectual centres of the various kingdoms, venerable texts such as the *Yi Jing* were reinterpreted. Confucian moralists concentrated on ethical issues reflected in the social content of the text. Daoists and *Yin-Yang* theorists were interested in cosmological issues suggested by the numerological and symbolic relations between the graphic matrices (McGreal, 1995: 63). Military strategists were interested in combining those elements into the formation of military strategies, so-called *Bing Fa*.

Bing Fa is a form of strategic thinking that was first developed for military purposes and has since been applied to almost all human interactions. The most influential *Bing Fa* was written by the master Sun Zi in the 4th century BC (Chu, 1995). In his book, *Sun Zi Bing Fa*, the author discusses the five elements that must be considered in formulating a strategy (Chu, 1995: 25–30):

1 The moral cause: The *Dao* addresses the morality and righteousness of a battle. This must be thoroughly understood by those who would affect the outcome.
2 Temporal conditions: Heaven is signified by *Yin* and *Yang*, manifested as summer and winter and the changing of the four seasons.
3 Geographical conditions: The earth encompasses far and near, danger and ease, open ground and narrow passes.
4 Leadership: The commander must be wise, trustful, benevolent, courageous and strict.
5 Organization and discipline: Organization and discipline must be thoroughly understood. Delegation of authority and areas of responsibility within an organization must be absolutely clear.

The harmony of the five elements is of great importance for success in any endeavour (Chu, 1995: 32). These are intangible, spiritual and psychological elements which are more related to the mindset rather than the hardware.

Another very different but influential philosophical thinking compared to Confucian and Daoist views is Legalism. This school of thought is a top-down philosophy and asserts that not all people are naturally good; some are bad and greedy (Watson, 1964). Therefore, the principles of the 'rule by law' and 'everyone is equal before the law' are the fundamental approaches of Legalism. The task of rulers, or leaders in terms of our current study, is to establish and maintain order by creating rules and regulations with efficient self-governing institutions to enforce rules through rewards and punishments, without exception, and to control the people (Watson, 1964). A Legalist leader can therefore be sharply contrasted with a Confucian leader, as the latter strives for harmony by practising benevolence, righteousness, eloquence and wisdom. A Legalist leader, however, seeks total obedience to the rule.

Whereas philosophers in most schools of thought are educated, the followers of Mohism are largely laypeople who advocate the equality of all social classes and promote heroism based on the spirit of *xia shi* (the Chinese equivalent of knights-errant). A Mohist leader (*ju zi*) is selected and judged by: 1) high ambitions; 2) bravery and courage; and 3) endurance of self-denial and austerity during salvation (Tan and Sun, 2009). Such perceptions of leadership were demonstrated in the history of Mohism, for instance, when Meng Sheng, a Mohist leader, committed suicide because he was unable to keep his promise to defend his friend's city. His 183 subordinates chose to follow their leader's example. Later, some say, Communist leader Mao Zedong adopted this theory of leadership to motivate the Communist Party to defeat Japan during World War II, advocating striving to win by setting goals, being prepared to sacrifice and tackling all obstacles (Lu, 2011).

From the above review, we can summarize the underlying elements that may be responsible for the development of modern managerial approaches in East Asia. The following key issues can be identified as the fundamental relational values which determined the formation of managerial knowledge based on the combination of Chinese traditional thinking, although this was not without disagreement:

- The establishment of the fundamental virtue of *Ren* (heartedness/benevolence) within the organization: Under such influence, the concepts of 'workplace is family' and 'bosses are parent figures' are widespread among Chinese and other East Asian organizations. Accordingly, the organization/ management is required to look after the interests of fellow employees, while employees have a strong commitment towards the organization. The outcome of implementing this relational virtue can be reflected in management and individual behaviours, and includes (from the management's side) employment security, compensation and a reward scheme, training (as part of educational function) and development (including promotion), It also includes strong commitment, self-discipline and a blurred time boundary between work and leisure (more overtime work) from the employees' side. The eventual goal of such efforts is to achieve a peaceful and orderly workplace with a social hierarchy and mutual support.

- Collectivism and interdependent relational value: This well-defined principle within Confucianism maintains that an individual is not an isolated entity. Therefore, the concept of family life as the basic unit in society is emulated within the work setting, and with it the broader societal values that ensure social harmony and behavioural ritual are preserved (Scarborough, 1998; Yau, 1988; Whiteley et al., 2000). Issues such as teamwork, sharing values and information, and group-oriented incentive schemes are very significant in daily activities. Hence, leader–follower exchanges with trust and reciprocity are fundamentals within an organizational and individual DNA.
- The doctrine of means – the harmony and the balance between *Yin* and *Yang*: The effort to achieve harmonization of workplace and maintain a dynamic reversion that perpetually counterbalances all propensities toward one extreme or the other places the organization in a stable and sustained position. The concept of *Yin* and *Yang* provides a mindset for coping with the environment in an adaptive and flexible way. Hence, for leaders and leadership styles, a balanced approach with flexibility is an important quality.
- Strategic thinking and strategic management: The everchangingness of internal and external factors forces human beings (both leaders and followers) to adopt strategic thinking in order to survive, not only in the short term but also in the long term. The outcome of combining different philosophies, such as *Bing Fa*, fulfils the needs of strategic thinking. The five elements of *Bing Fa* based on Confucianism, Daoism and *Yi Jing* provide general guidance for strategic thinking which helps organizations form business strategies with vision and clear goals.

Based on these principles, the quality of leadership vis-à-vis management needs to be investigated further (see Warner, 2014; Warner, 2016). In ancient China, the philosophical stance on leaders and leadership was more tolerant of ambiguity and elasticity: a single word, *ling dao*, was used as a noun, a verb or an adjective to describe a person (leader), a position (leader), a process (leadership) and a leader's attributes (Nisbett, 2003). The meaning of *ling dao* includes both 'leading' and 'directing'. Therefore, the theory of paternalistic leadership combining benevolence, morality and authoritarianism has been very influential in East Asia (Chen and Kao, 2009). A paternalistic leadership style is rooted in East Asia's historic patriarchal tradition, but less is known about whether it remains applicable during the current developmental stage.

In addition, the concept of *wu wei er zhi* (ruling effortlessly) is also a core theme of traditional thinking on rulers' governance, based on Daoism and a certain degree of Confucianism. This principle stresses the existence of a leader who does not actively intervene in the natural workings of production or the economy, or in the public sphere; and in this respect it could be said to have some elements in common with the *laissez-faire* doctrine in the West. The philosophy strives towards the balance of *Yin* and *Yang*, flexibility, adaptability and pragmatism, the influences of which are discernible in East Asian leadership practices (Ren et al., 2011).

However, these philosophies entail thoughts that are often different to each other, or even contradictory (e.g. Confucianism vs. Legalism). Therefore, a further examination of the influences of various schools of philosophy on leadership style during the political, social and economic transformational period is relevant and timely. This will be the major task of the case studies in the chapters that follow.

Comparative analysis of leadership concepts between East and West

It is important to compare and contrast the leadership concepts between East and West before we move on to the case studies in the following chapters. We can thus not only clarify some fundamental differences rooted in our thinking, but also provide logical understanding of the intertwined elements being adopted in current management and leadership practices.

Based on our reviews above, in particular regarding the early years of formation of leadership concepts, a fundamental characteristic emerging is that 'Western' thinking was rooted in individualistic behaviour of a leader or leadership position within an organizational environment. The major interaction between leader and others was based on the logic of transaction, regardless of whether it entailed the rationale of a leader's control or decision-making or of economic efficiency. In contrast, 'Eastern' thinking was rooted in the human relationship determinate; in other words, regardless of whether the relationship took place within a family or at a workplace, human engagement was based on an orderly and defined relationship, and each person was expected to behave and engage with the other accordingly. Parents at home or leaders in the workplace had to lead and guide by moral example and care; control may not have been necessary if all individuals were aware of their role in that relationship and acted accordingly. Such individually embedded roles and actions through education and awareness (e.g. Confucianism) could lead to *wu wei er zhi*. These different concepts can lead to different leadership outcomes, namely, control-oriented styles in the West vs. nurturing-oriented styles in the East. Although more recent leadership concepts in the West have moved away from control- and transaction-oriented approaches towards empowerment, transformational and even authentic-oriented approaches, some fundamental differences still exist, in particular with regard to routine management practices in reality.

By following the development of newer concepts of leadership in more recent years, we can see a trend towards a middle ground between East and

West emerging. For example, in East Asia many so-called Western concepts have been introduced and adopted in the workplace as part of the process of business and management in globalization practices. However, the combination of existing management practices in East Asian countries – whether in Japan and South Korea or China and Taiwan (see later chapters for details) – is being implemented with care. At the same time, many new concepts being developed in mainstream English literature on leadership have been included in relational-based approaches, emphasizing going beyond individualistic behaviour, but with more attention being paid to collective role and behaviour. With the emergence of authentic leadership, a combination of East and West elements – including flexible, situational, moral and transpersonal leadership quality – has been seen as a core value and a quality of a successful leader.

Alongside the increasing interplay between Western and Eastern business, trade and cultural exchanges, another distinctive pattern of leader behaviours emerges, termed paradoxical leader behaviour. This new concept describes encompassing seemingly competing yet interrelated leader behaviours so as to meet workplace demands simultaneously and over time (Zhang et al., 2015). Paradox is a key theme in the subsequent chapters of our book when we discuss in more detail the leadership challenges in the respective countries studied. From a theoretical point of view, paradoxical leader behaviours include five dimensions, namely:

1   combining self-centredness with other-centredness;
2   maintaining both distance and closeness;
3   treating subordinates uniformly while allowing individualization;
4   enforcing work requirements while allowing flexibility; and
5   maintaining control of decision while allowing autonomy.

(Zhang et al., 2015)

In a business environment where managers face intensified multiple demands, the practice of paradoxical leader behaviours satisfies implicit social expectations, and has the potential to reconcile the tensions and conflicts of different stakeholders.

As Chapter 1 indicated, this book examines the different ways in which business leaders improve their leadership competencies to navigate the complex and dynamic environments of the global economy. Therefore, a number of key questions will drive the following chapters to develop the argument with evidence:

- What are the traditional values and thinking influencing leaders' management and leadership practices?
- What has changed in terms of leadership concepts and practices influenced by 'Western' concepts under the process of globalization?
- What are the key concerns of business leaders in East Asia for confronting challenges and becoming successful and sustainable leaders?

So far, the underpinning philosophies and theories present an idealist way of leadership, but the reality could be different and we will observe these in the following case study chapters.

References

Banks, G. C., McCauley, K. D., Gardner, W. L. and Guler, C. E. (2016) 'A meta-analytic review of authentic and transformational leadership: A test for redundancy', *Leadership Quarterly*, 27: 634–652.

Bargh, J. A., Green, M. and Fitzsimons, G. (2008) 'The selfish goal: Unintended consequences of intended goal pursuits', *Social Cognition*, 26: 534–554.

Boekhorst, J. A. (2014) 'The role of authentic leadership in fostering workplace inclusion: A social information processing perspective', *Human Resource Management*, 54(2): 241–264.

Carter, D. R., DeChurch, L.A., Braun, M. T. and Contractor, N. S. (2015) 'Social network approaches to leadership: An integrative conceptual review', *Journal of Applied Psychology*, 100(3): 597–622.

Chen, H.Y. and Kao, H. S.R. (2009) 'Chinese paternalistic leadership and non-Chinese subordinates psychological health', *International Journal of Human Resource Management*, 20(12): 2533–2546.

Chrobot-Mason, D., Gerbasi, A. and Cullen-Lester, K. L. (2016) 'Predicting leadership relationships: The importance of collective identity', *Leadership Quarterly*, 25: 298–311.

Chu, C. N. (1995) *The Asian Mind Game: A Westerner's Survival Manual*, Crows Nest, NSW: Stealth Productions.

Coyne, S. (2017) 'Sustainable leadership: Rewire your brain for sustainable success', Transpersonal Leadership Series: White Paper Three, www.leadershape.biz/presenting-leadershaper [accessed on 25 March 2017].

Dansereau, F., Cashman, J. and Graen, G. (1973) 'Instrumentality theory and equity theory as complementary approaches in predicting the relationship of leadership and turnover among managers', *Organizational Behavior and Human Performance*, 10(2): 184–200.

Day, D. V. and Sin, H. P. (2011) 'Longitudinal tests of an integrative model of leader development: Charting and understanding developmental trajectories', *Leadership Quarterly*, 22: 545–560.

De Mente, B. (1994) *Chinese Etiquette and Ethics in Business*, Lincolnwood, IL: NTC Business Books.

Dehaene, S. (2014) *Consciousness and the Brain: Deciphering How the Brain Codes Our Thoughts*, New York: Penguin.

Dragoni, L. (2005) 'Understanding the emergence of state goal orientation in organizational work groups: The role of leadership and multilevel climate perceptions', *Journal of Applied Psychology*, 90: 1084–1095.

Fiedler, F. E. (1964) 'A contingency model of leadership effectiveness', *Advances in Experimental Social Psychology*, 1(1): 149–190.

Graen, G. and Uhl-Bien, M. (1995) 'Relationship-based approach to leadership: Development of leader-member exchange (LMX) theory of leadership over 25 years: Applying a multi-level multi-domain perspective', *Leadership Quarterly*, 6(2): 219–247.

Graham, J. W. (1991) 'Servant-leadership in organisations: Inspirational and moral', *Leadership Quarterly*, 2(2): 105–119.

Green, S. G. and Mitchell, T. R. (1979) 'Attributional processes of leaders in leader-member interactions', *Organizational Behavior and Human Performance*, 23: 429–458.

Hill, T. E. and Schmitt, N. (1977) 'Individual differences in leader decision making', *Organizational Behavior and Human Performance*, 19: 353–367.

Hill, W. A. and Hughes, D. (1974) 'Variations in leader behavior as a function of task type', *Organizational Behavior and Human Performance*, 11: 83–96.

Ibarra, H. and Barbulescu, R. (2010) 'Identity as narrative: Prevalence, effectiveness, and consequences of narrative identity work in macro work role transitions', *Academy of Management Review*, 35(1): 135–154.

Keller Hansbrough, T., Lord, R.G. and Schyns, B. (2015) 'Reconsidering the accuracy of follower leadership ratings', *Leadership Quarterly*, 26(2): 220–237.

Khatri, N., Ng, H. A. and Lee, T. H. (2001) 'The distinction between charisma and vision: An empirical study', *Asia Pacific Journal of Management*, 18: 373–393.

Kunda, Z. (1999) *Social Cognition: Making Sense of People*, Cambridge, MA: MIT Press.

Lord, R. G. and Brown, D. J. (2004) *Leadership Processes and Follower Self-Identity*, Mahwah, NJ: Erlbaum.

Lord, R. G., De Vader, C. L. and Alliger, G. M. (1986) 'A meta-analysis of the relation between personality traits and leadership perceptions: An application of validity generalization procedures', *Journal of Applied Psychology*, 71: 402–410.

Lord, R. G., Gatti, P. and Chui, S. L. M. (2016) 'Social-cognitive, relational, and identity- and based approaches to leadership', *Organizational Behavior and Human Decision Processes*, 136: 119–134.

Lowin, A. and Craig, J. R. (1968) 'The influence of level of performance on managerial style: An experimental object-lesson in the ambiguity of correlational data', *Organizational Behavior and Human Performance*, 3: 440–458.

Lu, Z. D. (2011) *Mao Zedong Ping Guo Xue (Mao Zedong's Comments on Chinese Classical Literature)*, Beijing: China International Culture Press.

Markus, H. and Wurf, E. (1987) 'The dynamics self-concept: A social psychological perspective', *Annual Review of Psychology*, 38: 299–337.

Martinko, M. J. and Gardner, W. L. (1987) 'The leader/member attribution processes', *Academy of Management Review*, 12: 235–249.

McGreal, I. (ed.) (1995) *Great Thinkers of the Eastern World: The Major Thinkers and the Philosophical and Religious Classics of China, India, Japan, Korea and the World of Islam*, New York: HarperCollins.

Naidoo, L. J. and Lord, R. G. (2008) 'Speech imagery and perceptions of charisma: The mediating role of positive affect', *Leadership Quarterly*, 19(3): 283–296.

Nisbett, R. E. (2003) *The Geography of Thought: How Asians and Westerners Think Differently … and Why*, New York: Free Press.

Oyserman, D., Elmore, K. and Smith, G. (2012) 'Self, self-concept, and identity', in M. R. Leary and J. P. Tangney (eds), *Handbook of Self and Identity*, New York: Guilford Press, pp. 69–104.

Ren, S., Zhu, Y. and Warner, M. (2011) 'Human resources, higher education reform and employment opportunities for university graduates in the People's Republic of China', *International Journal of Human Resource Management*, 22: 3429–3446.

Rindova, V. P. and Starbuck, W. H. (1997) 'Ancient Chinese theories of control', *Journal of Management Inquiry*, 6(2): 144–159.

Rockstuhl, T., Dulebohn, J. H., Ang, S. and Shore, L. M. (2012) 'Leader-member exchange (LMX) and culture: A meta-analysis of correlates of LMX across 23 countries', *Journal of Applied Psychology*, 97(6): 1097–1130.

Scarborough, J. (1998) 'Comparing Chinese and Western cultural roots: Why East is East and ...', *Business Horizons*, 41(6): 15–24.

Seers, A. (1989) 'Team-member exchange quality: A new construct for role-making research', *Organizational Behavior and Human Decision Processes*, 43(1): 118–135.

Sluss, D. M. and Ashforth, B.E. (2008) 'How relational and organizational identification es and converge: Processes and conditions', *Organization Science*, 19: 807–823.

Sluss, D. M., Ployhart, R. E., Cobb, M.G. and Ashforth, B. (2012) 'Generalizing newcomer's relational and organizational identifications: Processes and prototypicality', *Academy of Management Journal*, 55: 949–975.

Tan, J. J. and Sun, Z. Y. (2009) *Mo Zi Jin Zhu Jin Yi (The Current Notes and Interpretation of Moi Zi)*, Beijing: Commercial Press.

Walumbwa, F. O., Avolio, B. J., Gardner, W. L., Wernsing, T. S. and Peterson, S. J. (2008) 'Authentic leadership: Development and validation of a theory-based measure', *Journal of Management*, 34: 89–126.

Warner, M. (2014) *Understanding Management in China: Past, Present and Future*. London: Routledge.

Warner, M. (2016) 'Whither "Confucian management"?', *Frontiers of Philosophy in China*, 11: 608–632.

Watson, B. (1964) *Han Fei Tzu: Basic Writings*, New York: Columbia University Press.

Whiteley, A., Cheung, S. and Zhang, S. Q. (2000) *Human Resource Strategies in China*, Singapore: World Scientific.

Yau, O., (1988) 'Chinese cultural values: Their dimensions and marketing implications', *European Journal of Marketing*, 22(5): 44–57.

Zehnder, C., Herz, H. and Bonardi, J. P. (2017) 'A productive clash of cultures: Injecting economics into leadership research', *Leadership Quarterly*, 28(1): 65–85.

Zhang, Y., Waldman, D. A., Han, Y. L. and Li, X. B. (2015) 'Paradoxical leader behaviors in people management: Antecedents and consequences', *Academy of Management Journal*, 58(2): 538–566.

3 Business leaders and leadership in Japan

Introduction

Japan is an island country, with a relatively homogenous, stable and pluralistic society compared to other Asian economies. It is an archipelago stretching some 3,000 kilometres north to south, and covering an area of 378,000 square kilometres. According to the Global Competitiveness Report, the total population in July 2016 was 126.9 million – a fall of 0.28 per cent on the 2010 population figure (World Economic Forum, 2016). The majority of Japanese (more than 67 per cent) live in urban areas along the coast. Japan is the third largest economy in the world, achieving a total GDP of $4,123 billion in 2015 with a per capita of $32,485 (Table 3.1). Generally speaking, Japan is one of the richest countries in Asia and the world, with an annual disposable income of JPY313,380 per person. As a developed economy, Japan ranks sixth out of 140 countries in terms of competitive economy and seventeenth out of 136 countries among the most attractive investment markets. The country's ranking in terms of corruption is also relatively low at eighteenth out of 175 countries. In recent years, both inward and outward foreign direct investment (FDI) has declined, mainly due to an economic slowdown in Japan.

In recent years, perhaps for two decades, Japan has experienced a long period of economic stasis, with increasing pressure from financial deficit, low economic growth and an ageing population. Business leaders have been struggling to find ways to survive in such a tough environment. Given that Japan has a strong and unique cultural tradition and was influenced to a certain extent by the West, in particular the United States, during the post-WWII period, its leadership style has formed and re-formed over time with either Eastern or Western orientation under various economic, social and cultural circumstances. The recent field-trips in Japan by one of the authors found increasing frustration among Japanese leaders about fully adopting a Western style of leadership in their workplaces.[1] An obvious choice of action among business leaders is to promote momentum towards revitalizing Japanese business leadership by rebuilding its confidence through the adoption of hybrid systems which combine both Japanese and Western leadership styles.

Table 3.1 Economic, business and social indicators in Japan (2015–2016)

GDP in 2015 (US$ billion)	4,123	Disposable personal income in 2016 (JPY)	313,380
GDP per capita in 2015 (US$)	32,485	Employed workforce in 2016	64,460,000
Global competitive score in 2015 (1–7)	5.5	Corruption index in 2015 (1–100)	75
Global competitive rank in 2015 (out of 140)	6	Corruption rank in 2015 (out of 175)	18
Global opportunity score in 2015 (1–10)	7.23	FDI inward stocks by the end of 2015 (US$ billion)	202.5
Global opportunity rank in 2015 (out of 136)	17	FDI outward stocks by the end of 2015 (US$ billion)	1,259

Source: Japanese Trade and Investment Statistics 2016: www.jetro.go.jp/en/reports/statistics/.

This chapter aims to illustrate the key aspects of business leadership in Japan through the investigation of historical changes, cultural tradition and the impact of this tradition on business leadership, Western influence on business leadership, the tension between conventional practices and new challenges to change, and the issue of leader development. Finally, the chapter is concluded by identifying a number of implications for literature and practice.

Traditional normative values on leadership

Traditional normative values in Japan share some of their roots with Chinese traditional thought, such as Confucianism. In terms of faiths, the Japanese Shinto religion and Zen Buddhism have also had a profound impact on people's mind-sets, attitudes and behaviour (Kumon and Rosovsky, 1992). These religious and philosophical traditions emphasize the link between the current life and the next life, and teach people to be enlightened and well-behaved in order to achieve a better life in this life as well as the next one. Japanese social and cultural norms also emphasize social order and social hierarchy. However, in contrast to the Chinese, Japanese people are more accepting of their current social status and are committed to do well in their current positions. Without a history of political revolution as in China, people in Japan believe that social hierarchy is a natural thing and individuals should 'accept and obey'. By doing one's work well, everyone can obtain glory by achieving remarkable results and making a contribution to society.

Hence, Japanese people have a strong spirit of the 'tinkerer', doing things well with strong commitment, sincerity and passion (Kumon and Rosovsky,

1992). Most people see their jobs as long term with a life-time commitment. The leadership systems share some common characteristics with other East Asian economies, such as emphasis on hierarchy, paternalism, strong personal loyalty and commitment, and the importance of social networks in business and individual lives (Ren and Zhu, 2015). The belief system values harmony, uniformity and the tendency to see individuals in a socially dependent context.

In terms of traditional normative values on leadership, business leadership thought can be traced to its traditional philosophies with the most prominent influence of Confucianism. Fundamentally, Confucianism emphasizes social order and hierarchy as well as social relationships based on reciprocity. As discussed in the previous chapter, under the influence of Confucianism, respect for social order provides the rationale for individuals to perform their own work well, with commitment; but social hierarchy ensures that people obey the rules and observe social status. Given that social order requires individuals to do their work well with commitment, the spirit of the 'tinkerer' among business leaders enables them to lead by good example and consider customer satisfaction as the highest reward for their hard work (Austin, 2009). These qualities work together in reciprocal relationship-building which provides the foundation of productive business networks.

For many years, paternalistic leadership has been the dominating leadership style in Japan, as in other East Asian economies (Cheng et al., 2014). Reciprocal relationship-building in Japan is unique and is characterized by the concept of *Wa*, which refers to horizontal harmony in a group and collective responsibility. This concept differs from *Guangxi* in China and Taiwan, and from *Inhwa* in South Korea, which emphasize interpersonal connectedness including vertical differentiation (Cheng et al., 2014). However, there are some commonalities among these East Asian economies regarding leadership characteristics, including managers exhibiting some authority, leading by benevolent (*ren*) guidance, and setting a moral example (Farh and Cheng, 2000; Cheng et al., 2014). Comparative research between Australia, China and Japan by Sarros and Santora (2001) found that Japanese managers emphasized the collective good through their universalistic and benevolent approach. The value system is driven by attention to the needs of people rather than the push for money (Sarros and Santora, 2001: 247). In addition, the value orientation of security and the emphasis on harmony could be seen as the essential nature of Japanese leadership as a symbol of respect, guidance and consultation that underpin Confucian ideology (ibid.). Furthermore, Japanese leaders respond with paternalistic attitudes toward their employees, expressed by the philosophy of *mendou-miru*, which means 'I think about you; I will take care of you' (Dorfman et al., 1997: 237). In a hierarchical and ordered work environment, Japanese leaders generally give subordinates autonomy to achieve company goals, as reflected by the term *omakase*, which means 'I trust you and you can do it' (Sarros and Santora, 2001: 247).

However, if we look at these issues more deeply, authoritarian behaviours are evaluated differently among the various East Asian economies. In Japan, leaders treat employees more harshly if they do not meet targets or if they violate the principles compared to their counterparts in other East Asian economies. This attitude could be attributed to the fact that, in Japan, harmony is emphasized horizontally but not vertically, in comparison with China, Taiwan and South Korea (Cheng et al., 2014). In fact, the concept of discipline through criticism is related to a greater extent to the consciousness of shame (i.e. disapproval by others) rather than guilt (i.e. subject to discipline because of wrongdoing). Leaders are also likely to be reprimanded for a lack of control over their subordinates, just as leaders taking responsibility for a fault can be seen as a social norm (Swierczek and Onishi, 2003). In addition, Japanese leaders separate their 'public-self' from 'private-self'; namely, they behave in a more rigidly formal manner in public but are very frank and pleasant-mannered in a private environment (ibid.). Japanese subordinates are familiar with this kind of leadership behaviour, but it would be very hard for employees in other countries to understand and respond to such behaviour in the case of Japanese companies operating overseas under their internationalization strategy. Other relevant issues will be discussed in the next section in relation to the globalization and internationalization of Japanese business.

Influence of Western management practices

Since the end of WWII, Japan has experienced many complex political and economic developments with a strong North American influence (Kumon and Rosovsky, 1992). Many Western (or US) management concepts were introduced into a unique and relatively conservative social and cultural environment in Japan; these include Taylorism (see Warner, 1994) and Total Quality Management (TQM) systems based on the approach introduced by the US scholar W. Edwards Deming, 1982). In the area of business leadership, a number of concepts were introduced and gradually adopted in Japan under the influence of the globalization and internationalization of Japanese business, including transformational leadership, transactional leadership, charismatic leadership, situational leadership and ethical leadership (Bass, 1991; Fukushige and Spicer, 2007; Jung et al., 1995; Rao and Hashimoto, 1996; Sarros and Santora, 2001; Smith et al., 1989; Swierczek and Onishi, 2003; Yokochi, 1989).

As Yokochi's (1989) research demonstrated, Japanese leaders display more transformational leadership than transactional or laissez-faire leadership styles due to cultural factors. Culturally, Japanese leaders uphold humanistic values and high corporate goals (Yokochi, 1989: 196). They take full responsibility for organizational outcomes, and are likely to give concrete guidance to subordinates for their career development (Bass, 1991). In return, they receive high levels of respect and trust from their subordinates and make greater efforts to understand the feelings and needs of subordinates (Bass and Yokochi, 1991; Yokochi, 1989). In addition, in a collectivistic working environment, the Japanese share mutual interests and a sense of common fates with their organization (Triandis, 1994). Work teams have a more clearly delineated identity and a more homogeneous view of events than their counterparts in the West (Smith et al., 1989). Therefore, transformational leaders in this environment are more likely to motivate followers to work for transcendental goals instead of immediate self-interest. In return, followers are more easily motivated by leaders' inspirational behaviour (Jung et al., 1995). Based on this analysis, we can see that cultural elements play an important role in adopting and combining traditional values with Western concepts of leadership in practice.

In more recent years, there has been a trend to combine Western concepts and learning with a Japanese spirit in management practices (Hasegawa, 2010). In particular, certain Japanese companies focused on the internationalization of their businesses have tried to combine so-called 'American-style' rational business practices with Japanese business methods such as consolidated management, profitability-centre and cash-flow plan as core pillars of a turnaround effort to revitalize Japanese businesses domestically and internationally. A more individualistic approach, such as the 'three-self' concept – namely self-motivation, self-management and self-awareness – is also widely promoted in Japanese companies (Hasegawa, 2010).

Under the influence of globalization, more Japanese companies have developed business operations in other countries, and other foreign MNCs have also established their subsidiaries in Japan. Hence, there have been more opportunities for Japanese business leaders to work in diverse cultural environments. A number of studies have identified challenges presented by these circumstances. For example, the study by Rao and Hashimoto (1996) of Japanese expatriate managers in Canada demonstrated that they adopted hybrid management styles with Eastern and Western elements, including autocratic and assertive management as high-context Japanese culture, combined with greater direct interpersonal communication and interpersonal influence with Canadian subordinates as low-context Canadian culture. In addition, Japanese managers apply a greater degree of reason, using printed material, data and logic with Canadian subordinates in Canada, compared with the communication style in Japan, which applies less reason and provides less detailed information to Japanese employees.

However, in order for their internationalized business operations to be more successful in the future, there are many areas requiring further improvement. As Rao and Hashimoto demonstrated, language barriers appear to have a strong effect on communication and influence. A lack of subtlety in expression may lead to Japanese leaders appearing harsh and applying more assertiveness and sanctions. This manner could damage the long-term relationship between leaders and subordinate. In addition, Swierczek and Onishi's (2003) study of Japanese managers in Thailand also indicated that the senior leadership at their Thai subsidiaries generally lacks autonomy and flexibility to make decisions according to local situations; they also fail to encourage good behaviour, lack respect and are very harsh in their public criticism of Thai employees, who consequently feel shame, humiliation and embarrassment. Given that more Japanese companies are moving to off-shore operations, future development crucially requires more training in understanding different cultural environments, being flexible and adaptable, and enhancing capability-building in managing multicultural workforces.

Tensions

The debate on whether to maintain traditional Japanese leadership styles and management systems or fully adopting Western leadership styles and management systems has been evolving for decades, in particular since the early 1990s when the Japanese economy went into recession (Fukushige and Spicer, 2007; Hasegawa, 2010). The call for a full adoption of Western leadership/management systems was very loud in the 1990s, since most of the management institutes and think tanks in Japan and overseas blamed the traditional cultures and related leadership/management systems for causing the failure of business and economic performance among Japanese companies. This failure was labelled the 'end of Japanese style HRM' (Ornatowski, 1998). Under such influences, many Japanese companies tried to introduce and adopt Western concepts of leadership and management systems in the workplace. More importantly, after a number of leading Japanese companies were taken over by foreign (mainly Western) MNCs, such as Nissan, Western CEOs and senior management teams were brought into business operations in Japan (NissanNews.Com, 2016). These new teams started to implement their leadership and management systems in their business operations in Japan, and the results have been seen as more efficient and competitive than in the past (see Rowley et al., 2004).

However, the effect of adopting Western-oriented leadership and management systems into newly merged subsidiaries in Japan by Western MNCs is one thing; adopting them in indigenous Japanese companies in Japan is another. So far, such shifts towards Western systems among Japanese companies have not shown very positive outcomes. The criticism of blindly adopting Western systems in indigenous Japanese companies has increased in recent years and is seen in attitudes such as the disapproval of mimicking Western business models that emphasize speed and short-term results (Hasegawa, 2010). The most extreme view has been the call to revert to traditional Japanese business values and practices, including long-term orientation, attention to quality and detail, managing continuity and building consensus, steady-but-sure accretion of results (i.e. less risky), building constant improvement efforts, and developing technological and human assets (ibid.).

In interviews with 15 Japanese business leaders, Hasegawa identified the trend of adopting mixed leadership styles, with a combination of Eastern and

Western elements, in their day-to-day business operations in Japan. For example, business leaders became mindful of constant changes in their business environment, and then adopted situational leadership in order to meet such challenges, in particular in dealing with new risks. Other sentiments, such as 'don't simply imitate', 'don't be hampered by success', 'learn to read change' – which are completely counter to everything Japanese business leaders learned in the earlier years of their careers – started to fulfil the current leadership needs (Hasegawa, 2010: 22–23). However, with regard to the global challenges of an internationalization strategy, Japanese leaders became more aware of certain new principles, such as 'don't fall into conventional models', 'forget nationality, try universality', 'if you have clear objective, you will see plenty of opportunity', 'grow as locally as possible', and 'nothing great comes without putting yourself out there and taking a little risk' (Hasegawa, 2010: 73–75).

In recent years, business leaders – in particular those working in the new economic sectors such as IT and innovation – have become more tolerant towards failure than the previous generation. One business leader mentioned that 'business is always a sustained process of trial-and-error with limitless failures, and mistakes are part of business', and 'don't cover over failure, but treat it as a knowledge asset' (Hasegawa, 2010: 91).

Other elements include developing a new company culture by combining both old and new elements; shifting to a mind-set that views each employee as a protagonist; acting as an agent of change in times of economic and future instability; and setting goals towards which to strive and continually exceed (Hasegawa, 2010: 130). In addition, in terms of cultural tendency, new business leaders also challenge the traditional Japanese notion of 'not saying exactly what you mean'. Leaders believe that this attitude must change as companies expand globally and engage a more international workforce. Therefore, new business leaders must adopt an outward-looking business stance: never be satisfied with the status quo, but try to raise the bar as high as possible each day (Hasegawa, 2010:143).

The new elements of leadership style among the new generation of Japanese business leaders demonstrate unique combinations of leadership styles from both Eastern and Western concepts, with rational selection and adoption. The process of forming and re-forming leadership and management systems is a pragmatic evolution with constant adjustment. Based on observations during our fieldwork, we found that one of the key phenomena is the particular attention still paid by many Japanese business leaders to the principle of the spirit of the 'tinkerer', aiming to do things for themselves as leaders as well as for the employees who follow them, particularly among small and medium enterprises (SMEs), owners and managers and people with professional skills. Some common characteristics include persistence to achieve excellent results, paying attention to detail, dealing with complex issues with considerable patience, continuous exploration and innovation, ongoing learning and improvement, and always setting a good example for others to follow.

In recent years, due to changes in the economic climate, leader development
has become an important issue for business leaders in Japan in terms of continuous improvement in order to be able to maintain their leadership position.
Hence the following section will focus on the relevant issues.

Leader development

Business leader development in Japan can be divided into two major categories: a formal development process through the international labour
market; and an informal development process in family owned SMEs. With
regard to formal development, the process commences with the recruitment of
university graduates with basic degree qualifications. Once recruited, these
employees undergo a variety of training programmes both on and off the job,
although usually internal to the enterprise, over much of the course of their
employment (Benson, 2013). This skill acquisition, coupled with years of
experience with the enterprise, sees varying degrees of promotion and salary
increases. As a consequence, through the course of their employment and
training, most managers and senior executives become well integrated into the
enterprise and develop a strong loyalty to the firm. Those who perform at a
superior level ultimately gain promotions more rapidly and reach the higher
echelons of the enterprise (ibid.).

Generally speaking, three levels of managerial positions represent the
multi-leadership layers within companies: namely lower, middle and senior
levels. Lower-level supervisory managers are most likely to have entered the
enterprise directly from secondary school or vocational college. As such, their
chances of gaining senior management positions are relatively low (Benson,
2013). Upon recruitment, basic training is provided related to the use of particular machines, processes and systems, and job rotation through various
departments and jobs is accompanied by further training, which is usually in-
house and either on or off the job. If the recruits excel, they are promoted to
supervisory positions and some may move into middle management positions
with extra training (ibid.).

Middle managers are more likely to come from recruits who entered the
company with university degrees. In the first ten years or so these recruits
undertake job rotation and training courses conducted in-house (Benson,
2013). After the first few years employees displaying ability and talent begin
to gain promotion, and in so doing are given further training for their new
responsibilities. For many, a middle management position in a large company
is a satisfactory outcome. However, for those who are ambitious, undertaking
courses such as MBAs in their own time can gain them a promotion; or, in
the more likely case, changing employment either to a multinational cor-
poration or a smaller and less prestigious organization ensures them a higher
position. However, Japan has not relied on Western-style business schools but
has rather developed its own forms of business education for the most part
(see Warner, 1992; Warner, 1996; Warner, 2012).

Some middle managers reach top management levels. These managers have undergone similar training to the vast bulk of middle managers and, in addition, the promise they demonstrated in earlier stages of their careers identified them as being suitable for further training and development. Some of these managers may have undertaken higher levels of formal training or may have been sent overseas for training at prestigious institutions or to manage off-shore subsidiaries. More recently, major multinational companies such as Nissan and Sony have embarked upon advanced training programmes to enhance their global talent pool. These programs are characterized by the desire to bring more non-Japanese managers into the ranks of senior management as well as improve the availability of truly global managers. As such, these programs emphasize overseas placements, job rotations through various countries, training at elite business schools and bringing senior overseas managers to Japan (Benson, 2013).

A recent survey of leadership development in Japanese companies shows that the quality expected from employees in their rise to leadership within their organization is different between senior and middle level managers (Yuta and Yoshikazu, 2015). With regard to senior business leaders, 'leadership' entails creating a vision, disseminating the vision throughout the organization, and ensuring effective plans for succession (ibid.: 61). As for middle managers, they are expected to disseminate senior management's vision to their subordinates, and to implement this vision by managing their departments effectively and interacting with other departments (ibid.). In addition, young employees expect their leaders to be 'acting proactively', 'setting an inspiring example', 'taking initiatives, thereby setting an example for others', and 'getting things done by involving others' (ibid.: 62). In order to meet these expectations among the new generation of Japanese employees, Japanese companies have implemented new training initiatives, adding to their traditional methods. The focus is 'to develop people to lead our company', 'to heighten the ability to execute the company's vision and strategies', 'to motivate and strengthen trust relationship', and 'to develop people's leadership potential' (ibid.: 63). New training programmes include four key areas: authentic leadership training, facilitating leadership training, diversity leadership training and self-control training (ibid.). However, there are also some obstacles to developing leadership training programs; some of the main reasons include 'excessive budget requirements' and 'taking too much time' (ibid.).

In addition, women's leadership development is another area that has been gradually developed in recent years (Nezaki, 2014). Women's leadership has been a challenging issue in Japan given that the number of women managers was 9.1 per cent in 2005 and increased slightly to 10.6 per cent in 2010 (ibid.). A number of issues have been identified in Nezaki's study, including the need to train women leaders in effective time management and delegation skills, communication of team results, effective strategy and vision, seeking professional support from mentors and coaches, and avoiding career derailment. Hence, we can see from recent developments that leadership training in Japan has tackled a particular need for women's leadership, which is a positive sign in a traditionally patriarchal work environment.

Evaluation and conclusion

Japan has experienced dramatic changes, from high economic growth between the 1950s and 1980s to more than two decades of economic slowdown since the 1990s. The economic changes have also influenced the management/leadership thinking and practices from the adoption of Western (so-called 'new') management/leadership concepts and practices to the realization that copying the Western way is not good enough, leading to the adoption of more effective hybrid systems by combining Japanese and Western ways. The discussion in this chapter demonstrates the rationale for the shift. The momentum for revitalizing Japanese management/leadership systems is clearly derived from the rebuilding of leadership confidence by adopting a hybrid approach.

This chapter also demonstrates that the process of forming and re-forming management/leadership systems is a pragmatic evolution being constantly adjusted. However, one fundamental element which has not changed is that many Japanese business leaders still pay particular attention to the principle of the spirit of the 'tinkerer' to do things themselves as leaders (Kumon and Rosovsky, 1992). In addition, the internationalization of the Japanese economy also provides Japanese companies in general, and their business leaders in particular, with opportunities to learn a 'new' way of managing and leading business activities. Examples of these developments include the earlier years of overseas expansion by Japanese businesses which sent their leaders to head up operations overseas and learn the 'new' way; later foreign (mainly Western) MNCs moved into Japanese markets and brought the 'new' way into Japan (e.g. the case of Nissan).

Another important evaluation point is that the adoption of hybrid management/leadership systems is also influenced by the cultural context, as is seen in research by Jogulu (2009) which highlighted 'culturally linked leadership styles'. For example, Japanese business leaders could adopt transformative leadership, situational leadership and ethical leadership more easily than transactional or laissez-faire leadership styles due to their cultural links. This finding has a meaningful implication for management/leadership thinking as well as practices, in particular with regard to economies in a transitional stage.

The final but not least important point is related to the development of leaders. We have observed that Japan has a well-established and comprehensive leader development system. However, faced with new economic challenges, be it the economic slowdown or the pressure on internationalization – as well as the different expectations of capable leadership by the younger generation of employees – many Japanese companies have adopted new leadership training programs, adding to their established training systems. In addition, more leadership training programs have also been available for potential women business leaders; this is a positive move, indicating that Japanese company culture has shifted towards a combination of 'old' and 'new' elements of management/leadership systems. These new development phenomena will help us identify more meaningful implications in the final chapter of this book by comparing different case studies.

Note

1 Zhu carried out the fieldwork in Japan in January 2016 and April 2017.

References

Austin, U. (2009) 'Marketing Japan's travel and tourism industry to international tourists', *International Journal of Contemporary Hospitality Management*, 21(3): 356–365.

Bass, B.M. (1991) *Bass & Stogdill's Handbook of Leadership: Theory, Research and Managerial Implications*. New York: Free Press.

Bass, B.M. and Yokochi, M. (1991) 'Charisma among senior executives and the special case of Japanese CEO's', *Consulting Psychology Bulletin*, 1: 31–38.

Benson, J. (2013) 'Workforce development and skill formation in Japan: the shortcomings of an enterprise-based approach', in J. Benson, H. Gospel and Y. Zhu (eds), *Workforce Development and Skill Formation in Asia*, London and New York: Routledge, pp. 40–66.

Cheng, B.S., Boer, D., Chou, L.F., Huang, M.P., Yoneyama, S., Shim, D., Sun, J.M., Lin, T.T., Chou, W.J. and Tsai, C.Y. (2014) 'Paternalistic leadership in four East Asian societies: Generalizability and cultural differences of the triad model', *Journal of Cross-Cultural Psychology*, 45(1): 82–90.

Deming, W.E. (1982) *Quality Productivity and Competitive Position*. Cambridge, MA: MIT Press.

Dorfman, P.W., Howell, J.P., Hibino, L., Lee, J.K., Tate, U. and Bautista, A. (1997) 'Leadership in Western and Asian countries: Commonalities in effective leadership processes across cultures', *Leadership Quarterly*, 8(3): 233–274.

Farh, J.L. and Cheng, B.S. (2000) 'A cultural analysis of paternalistic leadership in Chinese organizations', in J.T. Li, A.S. Tsui and E. Weldon (eds), *Management and Organizations in the Chinese Context*, London: Macmillan, pp. 85–127.

Fukushige, A. and Spicer, D.P. (2007) 'Leadership preferences in Japan: An exploratory study', *Leadership & Organizational Development Journal*, 28(6): 508–530.

Hasegawa, Y. (2010) *Rediscovering Japanese Business Leadership: 15 Japanese Managers and the Companies They Are Leading to New Growth*, Singapore: Wiley.

Jogulu, U.D. (2009) 'Culturally-linked leadership styles', *Leadership & Organization Development Journal*, 31(8): 705–719.

Jung, D.I., Bass, B.M. and Sosik, J.J. (1995) 'Bridging leadership and culture: A theoretical consideration of transformational leadership and collectivistic cultures', *Journal of Leadership Studies*, 2(4): 3–18.

Kumon, S. and Rosovsky, H. (1992) *Political Economy of Japan: Cultural and Social Dynamics*, Stanford, CA: Stanford University Press.

Nezaki, H. (2014) 'Developing women leaders in Japan', *Training Journal*, 1 April 2014. www.trainingjournal.com/print/1366 (accessed 4 October 2016).

NissanNews.Com (2016) 'Carlos Ghosn: President and Chief Executive Officer Nissan Motor Co., Ltd', http://nissannews.com/en-US/nissan/usa/releases/carlos-ghosn (accessed 4 October 2016).

Ornatowski, G.R. (1998) 'The end of Japanese style human resource management?', *Sloan Management Review*, 39: 73–84.

Rao, A. and Hashimoto, K. (1996) 'Intercultural influence: A study of Japanese expatriate managers in Canada', *Journal of International Business Studies*, 27(3): 443–466.

Ren, S. and Zhu, Y. (2015) 'Making sense of business leadership vis-à-vis China's reform and transition', *Leadership & Organization Development Journal*, 36(7): 867–884.

Rowley, C., Benson, J. and Warner, M. (2004) 'Towards an Asian model of human resource management? A comparative analysis of China, Japan and South Korea', *International Journal of Human Resource Management*, 15(4/5): 917–933.

Sarros, J.C. and Santora, J.C. (2001) 'Leaders and values: A cross-cultural study', *Leadership & Organization Development Journal*, 22(5): 243–248.

Smith, P.B., Misumi, J., Tayeb, M., Peterson, M. and Bond, M. (1989) 'On the generality of leadership style measures across cultures', *Journal of Occupational Psychology*, 62: 97–109.

Swierczek, F.W. and Onishi, J. (2003) 'Culture and conflict: Japanese managers and Thai subordinates', *Personnel Review*, 32(2): 187–210.

Triandis, C.H. (1994) 'Cross-cultural industrial and organizational psychology', in M.D. Dunnette and L. Hough (eds) *Handbook of Industrial and Organizational Psychology*, Palo Alto, CA: Consulting Psychologists Press, pp. 103–172.

Warner, M. (1992) 'How Japanese managers learn', *Journal of General Management*, 17(3): 56–71.

Warner, M. (1994) 'Japanese culture, Western management: Taylorism and human resources in Japan', *Organization Studies*, 15(4): 509–535.

Warner, M. (1996) 'Culture, education and industry: managing management studies in Japan', in P. Joynt and M. Warner (eds), *Managing Across Cultures: Issues and Perspectives*, London: International Thomson Business Press, pp. 258–274.

Warner, M. (2012) 'Management education and training in East Asia: China, Japan and South Korea', in M. Warner (ed.), *Managing across Diverse Cultures in East Asia: Issues and Challenges in a Changing Globalized World*, London: Routledge, pp. 246–260.

World Economic Forum (2016) *The Global Competitiveness Report*. http://reports.weforum.org/global-competitiveness-report-2015-2016/economies/#indexId=GCI&economy=JPN (accessed 1 April 2016).

Yokochi, N. (1989) *Leadership Styles of Japanese Business Executives and Managers: Transformational and Transactional*, San Diego, CA: United States International University.

Yuta, M. and Yoshikazu, T. (2015) 'Actual condition survey of leadership development in Japanese companies', *Journal of International Business Research*, 14(3): 55–66.

4 Business leaders and leadership in South Korea

Introduction

South Korea (henceforth Korea), officially known as the Republic of Korea, is one of the first East Asian countries to have developed into an advanced economy (see Vogel, 1991). Along with Singapore, Hong Kong Special Administrative Region (SAR) and Taiwan, the country is known as an 'East Asian Tiger' for the rapid industrialization, economic growth and technological advancement taking place from the 1960s to the 1980s. Today Korea leads in high-technology exports and its gross domestic product (GDP), expressed in US dollars, ranked 11th globally in 2016 (Khoema, 2016).

With regard to its societal culture, Korea was considered one of the Confucian Asia Cluster countries in the Global Leadership and Organizational Behaviour Effectiveness (GLOBE) research project that investigated the interplay between culture, leadership and organizations across 61 countries. The Confucian Asia Cluster is characterized by collectivism (in-group and institutional) and performance orientation (Chhokar et al., 2012).

Correspondingly, the stereotypical view of Korea's managerial leadership is one that bears the legacy of Confucian normative values on team orientation, personal virtue, hierarchy and paternalism (House et al., 2004). While these endorsed leadership qualities are in line with the country's traditional culture, a challenge is presented by the fact that Korea has been undergoing significant economic, social and political changes since the mid-1980s. The dynamism experienced in Korea means that the research findings undertaken in the 1980s (e.g. House et al., 2004) need an urgent update to accommodate recent changes (Froese, 2013).

The aim of this chapter therefore is to outline Korea's managerial leadership and leadership development in transition through meaningful contextualization. The analysis is based upon interviews with local managers and expatriates in Korea, supplemented by relevant literature reviews.

Country context

Korea's economic history has resembled a roller-coaster, being marked by rapid industrialization since the 1960s, quick recovery of the failing growth after the 1997 Asian financial crisis, and recent slow-down in the aftermath of the global financial crisis, as well as the presidential crisis of 2016. Korea developed from a war-torn country, with GDP as low as US$67 in the 1950s, to a world leader in high-tech manufacture, with GDP soaring to US$1.378 trillion in 2015 (World Bank, 2016). Table 4.1 summarizes the country's key economic, business and societal indicators in 2015. Today, Korea is known for a number of high-tech brands worldwide that span various household products, such as Samsung and Hyundai. The country joined the Organisation for Economic Co-operation and Development (OECD) in 1996 and since accession its economic size has tripled, making it the 8th ranked member state in the OECD (Il-ho, 2016). This remarkable economic achievement is largely attributed to the far-reaching state interventions that created institutions to discipline both labour and capital (Kohli, 2004).

The so-called 'developmental state' stage started in 1965 when the export-oriented industries were promoted through state policies on tariff, exchange rates and subsidies (Froese, 2013). First, the state's intervention was critical because export-oriented technological development requires large-scale concentration beyond mere market forces. Second, the state suppressed trade unions and removed resistance to long working hours and low wages, thus providing a disciplined and cheap labour force (Koo, 2001).

Alongside export expansion, the state also facilitated structural changes in export composition. A key change was the shift from labour-intensive light industries to heavy and chemical industries (HCIs), which ultimately contributed to technology-intensive manufacturing (Gereffi and Wyman, 1990). This move was facilitated by the HCIs Plan (1973) under the leadership of President Park, who initiated a wide range of preferential policy treatments to industries such as automobiles, shipbuilding and electronics (Froese, 2013). President Park's policies also shaped the business landscape marked by a strong alliance between the state and big businesses. Despite a number of economic adjustment policies by the succeeding government to weaken this alliance, the state and big businesses remained intertwined (Rhee, 1994).

In recent years, Korea's global competitiveness has remained relatively unchanged, with a slight downward trend since 2007. In 2015, Korea ranked 26th globally according to the Global Competitive Report 2015–2016. Judged by its educational, labour market, financial, infrastructure and political institutions, Korea ranks 5th among Asian countries and the region in this report, after Singapore (2nd), and followed by Japan (6th), Hong Kong SAR (7th), Taiwan (15th) and China (28th). The country's capacity to retain talent and the relevance of pay to employee productivity is among the factors contributing to this global competitiveness. Nonetheless, Korea ranks extremely low out of the 140 countries in terms of hiring and firing practices (115th) and cooperation in labour–employer relations (132nd). This means that, from a business perspective, Korea's regulations are mostly seen as constraining flexible hiring and firing of employees. The conflict between worker and employer is also perceived as a concern in doing business in the country.

Table 4.1 Economic, business and social indicators in Korea in 2015

GDP (US$ trillion)	1.378	Average disposable income (US$)	29,016
GDP per capita (US$)	27,221	Corruption index (1–100)	56
Global competitive score (1–7)	4.99	Corruption rank (out of 168)	37
Global competitive rank (out of 144)	26	FDI inward stocks (US$ million)	174,573
Global opportunity rank (out of 136)	28	FDI outward stocks (US$ million)	278,395

Sources: World Bank, 2016; OECD, 2016; Corruption Perceptions Index 2015; Global Competitiveness Report 2015–2016; Global Opportunity Index 2015.

Korea's institutional conditions continue to make it an attractive destination for foreign direct investment (FDI). In this respect, according to the Global Opportunity Index, Korea ranks 28th out of 136 countries, due to the perceived quality of its labour force, legal infrastructure, ease of doing business and effectiveness of policymaking for trade and investment. The country's perceived level of public sector corruption in 2015, however, was only in the mid-range of the Corruption Perception Index score, slightly higher than in 2014.

Global ranking and scores, constructed in various ways via macro-economic prospects, labour market efficiency and institutional effectiveness, indicate that although Korea performs strongly compared to other Asian countries, there is concern over its long-term attractiveness to the global market. Korea is yet to leverage the full potential of its labour force and address policy stability. Other socio-economic issues include the slow growth of real wages, falling fertility rates and growing social distress (McKinsey, 2013a). Meanwhile, the domestic challenge is complicated by an increasingly competitive global market in which global recovery from the recent financial crisis is uneven. Within such a challenging and dynamic environment, we may ask: whither managerial leadership in Korea?

Traditional normative leadership values

Despite generally being seen as a Confucian society, Korea's traditional values and norms include a wide range of cultural and religious beliefs that have co-shaped the implicit mind-sets of society and the business community, the dominant philosophies being Buddhism and Confucianism.

Buddhism is the oldest established religion in Korea: introduced to the country in 372 during the three-kingdom period in early Korean history, it flourished during the Koryo dynasty (935–1392). Although Buddhism was persecuted in the succeeding neo-Confucian Choson dynasty (1392–1910) and experienced competition from other religious–philosophical systems during the period of Japanese colonialism and modernization to Western world systems, Buddhism scholars have remained robust in maintaining its relevance to help people cope with political, economic and societal changes (Wells, 2015).

A key tenet of Buddhism is that nature is interconnected with individuals and society (Park, 2010). In this vein, business leaders emphasize the unity of efforts among all relevant stakeholders in dealing with risks and threats. The function of leadership is to enable/assist others (e.g. employees) and produce goods/services needed for meaningful existence. A corollary of this dependent orientation is harmony, cooperation and working together for the collective good. So, at times a leader may implement decisions across the board that appear to be compulsory from the top.

Another key concept in Buddhism is humility, which is believed to liberate people from false perceptions about the world, the self and others. Humility is often expressed as being humble and genuine, with the realization that one is nobody. This realization of the 'emptiness' of one's ego reinforces the nature of interconnectedness (James, 1984). Working hard to practise unconditional love and compassion therefore becomes a valued work ethic.

Notwithstanding, the anti-materialist values of Buddhism also provide a spiritual balance to the hyper-competitive business environment with rising unemployment rates and social stress. Mindfulness as a Buddhist mediation practice has in recent years attracted people, including non-Buddhists, who seek to manage their feelings of stress and anxiety (Kim, 2016).

Influenced by Confucianism, as noted above, Korea is characterized by high power distance, acceptance of hierarchy, collectivism and strong male dominance (see Hofstede, 1980 and after). Within this culture, employees are seen as the most important stakeholders of an organization. This view does not focus on employees' contribution to organizations' productivity and profit, but rather sees employees as an end for which leaders have a duty of care (Witt and Stahl, 2016). Korea's national and organizational culture is family-oriented and emphasizes emotional harmony, hierarchy and seniority (Cho and Yoon, 2002). Correspondingly, managerial leaders are characterized as paternalist, autocratic and group-oriented.

The leadership style embedded in Confucianism manifests itself in Korean organizations in many ways, including the consciousness of hierarchy, the emphasis on seniority and the expectation of personal virtue. Hierarchy means Koreans are generally accepting of inequality of power. This high power distance culture paves the way for authoritarian managerial leadership in which top-down decision making is a key feature. While it may restrict flexible and open communication between leaders and non-leaders within the organization, the centralized decision making can have a positive influence on promoting efficiency, regulating behaviour and maintaining social order (Oh, 2003).

Leadership is determined by positional power, which in turn is defined by age, gender and social status (Cho and Yoon, 2002). In this context, seniority is favoured. Based on Confucian traditional values, employees are expected to demonstrate respect for and loyalty to elders or people in higher positions, and their experience. To some extent, seniority is a built-in virtue (Oh, 2003) that denotes one's commitment to the employing organization, and the possession of valuable firm-specific know-how. Correspondingly, seniority helps leaders gain respect and legitimacy from young employees; there is little resistance to seniority-based management systems (Chung et al., 1997). According to Business Demography Statistics in 2014 published by Statistics Korea, the one-year to five-year survival rate of active business is highly related to the age of CEOs. Businesses led by CEOs aged in their fifties and sixties performed better than the average survival rates. While explanations abound, this finding suggests the advantages associated with seniority.

Centralized authority and vertical hierarchical management do not mean that relationships between leaders and subordinates are one-way, with obligations of loyalty and deference going upwards only. Leaders are expected to practise personal virtue and work for the group. During our interviews, we asked participating managerial leaders to list qualities that they deem most essential for effective performance of everyday leadership roles. Apart from those discussed frequently in the mainstream English literature, diligence is also at the top of the list. Diligence is a highly valued virtue for Korean workers, including managerial leaders. Overtime work at night and weekends is an implicit norm in the work force. Our interviewees explained that they perceived organizational contexts to be competitive and that to perform competently, or at least to be perceived to perform competently, they needed to sacrifice personal leisure or family time for work.

Personal virtue is not necessarily equivalent to the Western concept of ethical leadership. The basic unit in Confucian traditional values is the family, and social relations are seen as an expansion of relationships in the family (Lee, 1998). This expansion is further reinforced by the social structure in Korea in which there are almost no racial or ethnic minorities that could lead to the disaggregation of conflicting groups (Lee, 1998). The emphasis on family values therefore sets it apart from ethical leadership that is fundamentally built on the atomistic view of the world in the West. For instance, the 1997 Asian financial crisis led leaders in large conglomerates to introduce notions of corporate social responsibility to restore their damaged reputation. However, a large survey of 147 Korean businesses recently undertaken by Shin and colleagues (2015) failed to find a direct relationship between ethical leadership at the top and financial performance at the firm level. While the relatively low appreciation of ethical leadership may be an explanation, the finding may also be attributed to the varying understanding of what makes leadership ethical in Korea compared to the West. We will turn to this in detail in the later part of this chapter when we discuss key tensions associated with practising business leadership in Korea.

In addition, the internalized moral perspective of a Korean traditional leader is a process of cultivating the mind and internal piety to achieve integrity (Kim

et al., 2015). This is a process of self-leadership which entails a profound understanding of one's purpose, strengths and limitations. Moral justice also requires
understanding subordinates' thoughts, perspectives and needs. So, morality is not
a closed view of humanity, but rather considers role-modelling embedded in
personal relationships as affecting others, and hence society.

In Confucian terms, the ultimate goal of leadership is to achieve *inhwa*
(harmony) between leaders and subordinates (Chen, 1995). Interpersonal
relationships are an important element in cultivating harmony in Korea.
Managerial leaders are expected to demonstrate empathy with their subordinates and keep the needs and feelings of these subordinates in mind. This
behavioural practice is expressed in Korea as *jeong*, defined as 'a bond of
affection or feelings of empathy to others' (Yang, 2006, p. 285). The introduction and interpretation of Confucianism in Korea emphasized an emotional view of the world with attention to the specific issues of human feelings
(Chen, 1995).Humanity's *jeong* comprises seven specific emotions: namely,
happiness, anger, worry, sadness, joy, hate and fear (Yang, 2006). In order for
a harmonious relationship to hold, the positive or warm emotions are
important. The affective bond of *jeong* does not apply only to the particular-
istic tie between managerial leaders and specific subordinates; it also extends
to the *woori* (i.e. collective) in which members of the collective group share
interdependence and emotional support (Yang, 2006). Therefore, managerial
leaders are expected to interact with their subordinates beyond work domains
and have a good long-term relationship with them.

While Korea shares a Confucian heritage with many other East Asian
countries, the country demonstrates its own characteristics. Prior research that
compares Korea with China and Japan (Froese, 2013) shows that the Chinese
are more individualistic and career oriented, whereas the Japanese are more risk-
averse and work oriented, with the Koreans in-between. Differences in the
endorsed values are a product of the macro-economic development of each
country relative to others. A general understanding is that individualism
increases with economic growth because, in developed economies, people are
less concerned with survival, but more with individualistic interest and growth
(e.g. Hofstede, 2001). China's noticeable economic growth is expected to
result in more realistic Chinese managers than those in Korea or Japan.

Additionally, managers in Korea show a higher level of acceptance of risks
and innovation compared to their counterparts in Japan. Shim and Steers
(2012) undertook a comparative study of leadership in Hyundai and Toyota,
and suggested that the frequent changes in executive personnel of Hyundai
were intentional so as to keep the organization 'on edge'. Nevertheless,
leadership in Toyota stresses stability, predictability and risk minimization.

Influence of Western management practices

Korea's management practices have been strongly influenced by the West,
particularly the US, which has close economic, political and military

engagement in the country. For instance, there is a long-standing partner relationship between Daewoo and General Motors, Kia and Ford. The business landscape is further influenced by the International Monetary Fund (IMF), from which Korea received aid during the Asian financial crisis in 1997. At the IMF's request, for instance, Korea amended the Korean Labour Standard Act so that employers could terminate employment contracts against the will of employees in special circumstances – namely financial deterioration, structural adjustment, technical innovation and change of business for productivity enhancement (Lee et al., 2013).

Since the mid-1990s, Korea has followed typical Western management practices, such as performance-based pay, which in turn influences managerial leadership styles. A recent study undertaken by Hamlin and colleagues (2016) reports a high degree of overlap between the effective managerial leadership behaviours of the Korean samples (87.75 per cent) and those of British samples (90.53 per cent). Managers in the private sector are expected to follow Western-based democratic practices which are closely linked with transformational leadership, such as open communication, participative management and the pursuit of consensus, but in reality fall short of the task. By comparison with other Asian counterparts, Korean leaders are relatively more straightforward, independent and individualistic (Morrison and Conaway, 2006).

Nonetheless, the history of fighting Japanese colonization and Western invasion contributes to a pride in Koreans' own national identity. The Confucian and Buddhist traditions mean that Koreans think and act associatively, relationally and subjectively (Morrison and Conaway, 2006). A cross-cultural study undertaken by Lee and colleagues (2014), for instance, found that Korea is only moderately collectivist, rather than extremely collectivist, as assumed in the GLOBE study. These authors go on to claim that Korea now has a hybrid culture due to globalization.

The interplay between Korean traditional culture and Western influences is complex. The adoption of Western practices is culturally shaped. Changes in employment management practices, for instance, are met with strong resistance in a seniority-dominated culture. Western practices are often adapted to suit the local organizational environment and commitments (Kim, 2015). Nonetheless, authoritarian and top-down leadership style remains largely unchanged. There is a good deal of evidence that this remains the case. Indeed, although corporate governance institutions exist in Korea, they are not well established or take a significant role as in Western countries. The major decisions, for instance, to diversify into different industries, are often encouraged by the government. Not surprisingly, senior leaders of Korean family-based conglomerate *chaebols* have reported official corruption within the government that reaches into their business.

The complexity is further reflected in the demographic changes in society. The number of foreigners residing and working in Korea is on the rise. Based on the 2016 Foreigner Labour Force Survey published by Statistics Korea, in

May 2016 there were 962,000 employed foreigners, up by 2.6 per cent from 2015. On the surface, the growing number of economically active foreigners facilitates the interaction between traditional cultures and Western ones. A break-down of employed foreigners by nationality shows that Asians make up approximately 60 per cent, with Korean Chinese totalling 45.9 per cent, followed by Vietnamese (7.4 per cent) and non-Korean Chinese (6.6 per cent). Foreigners from North America amounted to only 4.7 per cent. This means the everyday activities affected by cultural interactions, if any, are still largely Confucian in nature.

Tensions

The 'economy-first mentality' has contributed largely to rapid economic growth in the country; however, it leaves ethical dilemmas in the business sector and the society at large. The alliance between the government and big businesses, coupled with the importance of Korean conglomerates to the economy, means that the violations of laws and regulations by these businesses or their prominent leaders do not come with harsh punishments (Kim and Park, 2013). The most recent presidential scandal at the time of this publication, for instance, involves major conglomerates, which, albeit under pressure, improperly contributed to the foundations of President Park Geun-hye's confidante, Choi Soon-sil, in exchange for special treatment by the government. At the centre of this scandal is an investigation as to whether the approved merger between Samsung C&T Corp and Cheil Industries in 2015 was due to Samsung's relationship with the government, at the expense of other shareholders. Samsung is not the only *chaebol* investigated over the presidential scandal – the Lotte Group has also been affected. It is also not the first time that leading conglomerates are reported to have been guilty of misconduct in various realms, such as tax evasion, breach of duty and corruption. With the development of civil society, the public is increasingly dissatisfied with these wrongdoings, thus emphasizing the need to question the legitimacy of these conglomerates. Managerial leaders, particularly those at the senior and top levels, face the challenges of growing their business on one hand and managing relationships with the government on the other. This is not just a business issue, but also a moral one that involves a wider range of stakeholders, such as the general public.

Additionally, the extent to which Western practices enter into the implicit mind-sets of local managers is influenced by the unique characteristics of Korea's economic and political set-up. As mentioned above, Korea's economy is heavily dominated by big businesses (*chaebols*) with the aid of the government. This means the small and medium-sized enterprises (SMEs) are struggling to survive and find it difficult to grow into large businesses. McKinsey (2013a) estimated that SMEs operating only in the service industry contributed only 35–40 per cent to the productivity of Korean conglomerates. This is partly due to the lack of government support and partly due to the lack of laws and regulations to protect non-*chaebol* businesses. The transaction relationship between small businesses and *chaebols* is characterized by a low level of trust, much lower than in Japan and even slightly lower than in the US (Dyer and Chu, 2000). As a result many small business leaders have to cultivate personalized relationships (*jeong*) to win trust and obtain competitive advantage for their businesses. Not surprisingly, despite exposure to Western practices, personal relationship-building is still pervasive.

Rooted in the traditional collective orientation, relationship-building forms an important part of our interviewees' daily activities. Correspondingly, the lines between work domain and personal life are very blurred. Korea's society places a high emphasis on professional success as a sign of achievement in life. Managerial leaders, particularly men, have therefore put less value on maintaining a work–life balance. Our interviewees indicate that working hard is a virtue that helps them gain respect. Indeed, Korea has the longest working hours among OECD countries (Cho et al., 2015). On-site visibility is a key feature of Korean's leadership compared to other Asian countries (Shim and Steers, 2012). The prioritization of work over family is also in part due to the social practice of building personal relationships, which is often undertaken beyond work hours.

Progress of women's participation in leadership is slow. Korea performs badly in terms of gender-based disparities, ranking only 116th out of 144 countries in the *Global Gender Gap Report* 2016 (World Economic Forum, 2016). In the combined evaluation of female labour force participation – including in professional and technical work, and gender-based wage equality – Korea ranks even lower (123rd). This positions Korea well below other Asian counterparts such as the Philippines, Lao PDR, Singapore, Vietnam, Thailand, Indonesia, Malaysia, Japan and China. Only a very small proportion of women can break the so-called glass ceiling and make it to top leadership positions. In 2011, 48 per cent of university graduates were female, in turn occupying 40 per cent of entry-level professional work. However, only 6 per cent moved into middle- to senior-management positions, with even fewer in executive committees (2 per cent) or on boards (1 per cent) (McKinsey, 2013b).

The gender challenges in Korea's workplace are heavily shaped by the country's societal culture, endorsed both by men and women. Confucianism generally places women in an inferior status to men, and emphasizes their domestic responsibility (Kim and Rowley, 2009). During our interviews, we were informed that many women would leave their jobs voluntarily for family commitments after they get married or have children. Our male interviewees also considered that women were not suitable to undertake heavy job duties in leadership roles. Within such an environment, where the traditional culture does not effectively support women's career development, women who remain in the workplace have to deal with challenges both from work and from society. While women's economic contribution to the family and the economy are appreciated, raising children is still seen as their most important responsibility.

The low representation of women in leadership roles is not just a product of cultural barriers, gender discrimination or social pressure. The government and employers are also seen as not effectively helping women return to work (McKinsey, 2013a). The key family-friendly legislative changes promoted by the government are the extended paid maternity leave from 60 days to 90 days in the Labour Standard Act 2001 and parental leave-related stipends in the amendment to the Equal Employment Act. However, these policies raise concerns about the increasing cost to businesses and women's contributions to the organizations' performance (Bae and Goodman, 2014).

Women who eventually return to work are often unable to find high-quality jobs that match their education and previous work experience. Female leaders who remain in the workplace and perform well are reported to struggle for a balance between work and life. Cho et al. (2015) undertook an in-depth study with 18 female leaders holding general manager, executive or CEO positions in challenging workplaces. According to these women, the intrinsic commitment to work is the primary reason for them remaining in this role beyond the stereotypical view of women. However, what is typically expected of them as women is assessed by the academic achievements of their children. When these women had to return to work, the support they obtained was mainly from the family, such as grandmothers. It is evident that there is a growing need for more organizational and social support, such as flexible working hours.

Leader development

Training institutions in Korea that influence general mind-sets and behaviours, including leadership, are attributed with 'Korean' characteristics. Apart from the conventional form of business leader training, the mandatory military service, applied to male adults, contributes to ideas of how organizations should be designated and managed (Cho and Yoon, 2002). This training experience reinforces the emphasis on hierarchical order, orientation towards results and aggressive competition on a large scale.

Business leader development shows a changing pattern in Korea. Traditionally, it is heavily associated with intensive on-the-job training provided by the organizations in which employees stay to build their careers over the long term (Kim and Kim, 2003). However, a number of labour market changes have challenged this organization-dominated developmental mode. The first change is the transformation of human resource management (HRM) practices from seniority-based and lifetime employment-oriented to US-type, market-based approaches. There is thus growing emphasis on individual competence and performance, rather than a sole focus on employee loyalty and commitment (Choi et al., 2012). The best-known Western-style business schools are public institutions such as Seoul National University (SNU) and KAIST College of Business (KCB) at Korea Advanced Institute of Science and Technology. There are also seven private schools: Yonsei School of

Business (YSB) 10 at Yonsei University, Korea University, Sejong University, Sogang University, SungKyunKwan University, Hanyang University and Ewha Woman's University. Yonsei has been offering management studies since 1915. Its Global MBA Programme was launched in 1998 as the first English-only course in the country (see Warner, 2011).

The seniority-based, lifetime employment model was established during the 25-year military reign prior to 1987 when the government took an active role in shaping economic development, characterized by neo-mercantilism (Bae, 2011). The emphasis on work ethic and learning is a key feature of this employment model. With the end of the military reign, President Roh Tae-woo introduced the 'Democracy Declaration' in 1987, which encouraged political democratization and industrial restructuring. To accommodate these changes, Korean businesses experimented with a number of new practices referred to as 'New HRM'. The New HRM practices pluralized the developmental opportunities for managerial leaders, making tenure not the only determining factor for employees to climb up the management hierarchy. Fast-tracking promotion based on competencies, the provision of career development plans and training programmes in overseas universities were now available (Bae, 1997).

A more flexible, neo-liberal employment system emerged after the 1997 Asian financial crisis, resulting in shorter stays with the employing organization. Organizations increased their focus on developing professionals rather than generalists (Bae and Rowley, 2001). They also placed a high emphasis on developing and retaining talent; Bae (2011, p. 589) noted:

> Since the financial crisis, Korean firms have engaged in a war for talent and made greater effort to retain those people hired. Big corporations in Korea have always spent huge sums of money to attract the best people. But since the financial crisis, firms have been recruiting the best people even more aggressively. The organizations that have dashed into this war for talent include major business groups such as Samsung, LG Electronics, Hyundai Motor, SK, Hanwha, Doosan, and Kumho. For example, Lee Kun-hee the chairperson of Samsung declared that attracting and developing top talent would account for about 40 per cent of the performance evaluations of the CEOs of Samsung-affiliated companies.

The number of employees on flexible contracts (e.g. temporary or daily employees) has been on the rise, amounting to 6,682,000 in November 2016. Correspondingly, the responsibility for developing leadership competencies started to shift to individual managers. However, the young generation in Korea demonstrates a lower tendency towards an entrepreneurial spirit, compared to other Asian countries such as China or other OECD member states. This trend is present against the backdrop of an export-led growth model, which means that big conglomerates hire fewer employees at home, although they are expanding globally. The conglomerates' share of domestic employment is as low as 12 per cent (McKinsey, 2013a). Finding ways to revitalize the labour market, as well as the entrepreneurial mind-set of the young generation, therefore presents an urgent challenge to Korea.

Another implication of changing employment systems relates to the diversification of developmental methods. A Delphi study undertaken by Choi and colleagues (2012) demonstrates that the most effective developmental method for leaders at the middle level is establishing a task-force team, followed by coaching, 360-degree feedback, action learning and simulation. A task-force team has been particularly effective to develop leadership competencies related to performance management and teamwork building. As for those at the executive level, coaching is found to be the most effective developmental method (particularly for developing vision identification and formulation), followed by 360-degree feedback, action learning and job rotation. Interestingly, although the studied organizations provided access to MBA programmes, they were not perceived to be effective in developing leadership competencies either for middle- or executive-level managers. This is because effective leadership competencies in Korea require relationship and experience-based developmental methods rather than academic-based learning.

Evaluation and conclusion

History and path dependence have shaped the way effective leadership is perceived and practised in Korea. The country is influenced by the traditional religious and philosophical systems from neighbouring countries (e.g. China, Japan), which in turn evolved to cope with economic and societal transformation during the Japanese colonization, US aid and the more recent globalization. The traditional values of hierarchy, harmony and collectivism require managerial leaders to practise authoritarian leadership, even in their overseas subsidiaries. The institutional set-up of *chaebols* means senior leaders need to develop and maintain close ties with government leaders, often blurring the lines between business ethics and corruption. A state-intervened capitalism focused on export-oriented manufacturing has contributed much to Korea's rapid industrialization; however this growth formula does not seem as robust as most would expect in order to address recent challenges brought about by domestic socio-economic changes and global competition. Within such a context, effective managerial leadership shows both change and continuity in terms of style, practice and mind-set. Collectivism, strong male dominance, a gender-divided family structure and authoritarian management are still as relevant in today's Korea as they were in the past due to the pervasive traditional values. Nonetheless, the growing discontent with business scandals and the decreasing entrepreneurial momentum send an alarming signal to businesses and their leaders about the way ahead for Korea's economy and society. There is a need to transform the norm of personal virtue with diligence to organization-based ethical conduct and behaviour.

In summary, managerial leadership in Korea faces unprecedented challenges in terms of how leadership should develop. Western models have partially been absorbed, as noted above. Mandatory military service also reinforces hierarchy, order, competition and result-orientation within the body of Korean society (mainly male). The indigenous values of Korean management still prevail. Nonetheless, diversified developmental methods have emerged to accommodate the needs of the labour market. To sustain Korea's growth, developing a competent, resilient and gender-balanced leadership pool will be the key.

References

Bae, J. (1997) 'Beyond seniority-based systems: A paradigm shift in Korean HRM?', *Asia Pacific Business Review*, 3(4): 82–110.

Bae, J. (2011) 'Self-fulfilling processes at a global level: The evolution of human resource management practices in Korea, 1987–2007', *Management Learning*, 43(5): 579–607.

Bae, K. B. and Goodman, D. (2014) 'The influence of family-friendly policies on turnover and performance in South Korea', *Public Personnel Management*, 43(4): 520–542.

Bae, J. and Rowley, C. (2001) 'The impact of globalization on HRM: The case of South Korea', *Journal of World Business*, 36(4): 402–428.

Chen, M. (1995) *Asian Management Systems*, New York: International Thomson Business.

Chhokar, J. S., Brodbeck, F. C. and House, R. J. (eds) (2012) *Culture and Leadership Across the World: The GLOBE Book of In-Depth Studies of 25 Societies*, New York: Routledge.

Cho, Y., Kim, N., Lee, M. M., Lim, J. H., Han, H. and Park, H. Y. (2015) 'South Korean women leaders' struggles for a work and family balance', *Human Resource Development International*, 18(5): 521–537.

Cho, Y. H. and Yoon, J. K. (2002) 'The origin and function of dynamic collectivism: An analysis of Korean corporate culture', in C. Rowley, T. W. Sohn, and J. S. Bae (eds), *Managing Korean Business: Organisation, Culture, Human Resource and Change*, London: Frank Cass, pp. 70–88.

Choi, M., Yoon, H. J. and Jeung, C. W. (2012) 'Leadership development in Korea: A delphi study', *Asia Pacific Journal of Human Resource*, 50: 23–42.

Chung, K. H., Lee, H. C. and Jung, K. H. (1997) *Korean Management: Global Strategy and Cultural Transformation*, Berlin: Walter de Gruyter.

Dyer, J. H. and Chu, W. (2000) 'The determinants of trust in supplier-auto maker relationships in the U.S., Japan, and Korea', *Journal of International Business Studies*, 31(2): 259–285.

Froese, F. J. (2013) 'Work values of the next generation of business leaders in Shanghai, Tokyo and Seoul', *Asia Pacific Journal of Management*, 30: 297–315.

Gereffi, G. and Wyman, D. (eds) (1990) *Manufacturing Miracles: Paths of Industrialization in Latin America and East Asia*, Princeton, NJ: Princeton University Press.

Hamlin, R. G., Kim, S., Chai, D. S., Kim, J. and Jeong, S. (2016) 'Perceived managerial and leadership effectiveness within South Korean and British private companies: A derived etic comparative study', *Human Resource Development Quarterly*, 27(2): 237–269.

Hofstede, G. (1980) *Culture's Consequences: International Differences in Work-Related Values*, London: Sage.

Hofstede, G. (2001) *Culture's Consequences: Comparing Values, Behaviors, Institutions, and Organizations across Nations*, Thousand Oaks, CA: Sage.

House, R.J., Hanges, P.J., Javidan, M., Dorfman, P.W. and Gupta, V. (2004) *Culture, Leadership and Organizations: The GLOBE Study of 62 Societies*, Thousand Oaks, CA: Sage.

Il-ho, Y. (2016) 'Marking 20 years at the OECD: A new way forward' *OECD Observer*. http://oecdobserver.org/news/fullstory.php/aid/5646/Marking_20_years_at_the_OECD:_A_new_way_forward.html [accessed on 20 May 2017].

James, W. (1984) *The Varieties of Religious Experience*, New York: Random House.

Khoema (2016) *World GDP Ranking 2016*. https://knoema.com/nwnfkne/world-gdp-ranking-2016-data-and-charts-forecast [accessed on 20 March 2017].

Kohli, A. (2004) *State-Directed Development: Political Power and Industrialization in the Global Periphery*, Cambridge: Cambridge University Press.

Kim, D.O. and Kim, S. (2003) 'Globalization, financial crisis, and industrial relations: The case of South Korea', *Industrial Relations*, 42(3): 341–367.

Kim, D.M., Ko, J.W. and Kim, S.J. (2015) 'Exploring the ethical aspects of leadership: From a Korean perspective', *Asian Philosophy*, 25(2): 113–131.

Kim, H.M. (2016) 'Becoming a city Buddhist among the young generation in Seoul', *International Sociology*, 31(4): 450–466.

Kim, J., and Park, K. (2013) 'Ethical modernization: Research misconduct and research ethics reforms in Korea following the Hwang affair', *Science and Engineering Ethics*, 19: 355–380.

Kim, N., and Rowley, C. (2009) 'The changing face of Korean women managers', in C. Rowley and Y. Park (eds), *The Changing Face of Korean Management*, London: Routledge, pp. 184–209.

Kim, Y. (2015) 'Introduction to contemporary practice of performance management and measurement systems in Korea', *Public Performance & Management Review*, 39: 273–278.

Koo, H. (2001) *Korean Workers*, Ithaca, NY: Cornell University Press.

Lee, D., Kim, K., Kim, T.G., Kwon, S. and Cho, B. (2013) 'How and when organizational integration efforts matter in South Korea: a psychological process perspective on the post-merger integration', *International Journal of Human Resource Management*, 24(5): 944–965.

Lee, H. C. (1998) 'Transformation of employment practices in Korean businesses', *International Studies of Management & Organization*, 28(4): 26–39.

Lee, K., Scandura, T.A. and Sharif, M.M. (2014) 'Cultures have consequences: A configurable approach to leadership across two cultures', *Leadership Quarterly*, 25: 692–710.

McKinsey (2013a) *Beyond Korean Style: Shaping a New Growth Formula*. file:///C:/Users/Li/AppData/Local/Temp/MGI_Beyond_Korean_style_Full_report_Apr2013.pdf [accessed on 20 March 2017].

McKinsey (2013b) *Women Matter: An Asian Perspective*. file:///C:/Users/Li/AppData/Local/Temp/2012-McKInsey-Women-Matter-An-Asian-Perspective-1.pdf [accessed on 20 March 2017].

Morrison, T. and Conaway, W.A. (2006) *Kiss, Bow, or Shake Hands*, Avon, MA: Adams Media.

Oh, M.S. (2003) 'Study on appropriate leadership pattern for the Korean church in postmodern era', *Journal of Asian Mission*, 5(1): 131–145.

Park, J.Y. (ed.) (2010) *Makers of Modern Korea Buddhism*, New York: State University of New York Press.

Rhee, J.C. (1994) *The State and Industry in South Korea: The Limits of the Authoritarian State*, London and New York: Routledge.

Shim, W.S. and Steers, R.M. (2012) 'Symmetric and asymmetric leadership cultures: A comparative study of leadership and organizational culture at Hyundai and Toyota', *Journal of World Business*, 47(4): 581–591.

Shin, Y., Sung, S.Y., Choi, J.N. and Kim, M.S. (2015) 'Top management ethical leadership and firm performance: Mediating role of ethical and procedural justice climate', *Journal of Business Ethics*, 129: 43–57.

Vogel, E. (1991) *The Four Little Dragons*, Cambridge, MA: Harvard University Press.

Warner, M. (2011) 'Management education and training in East Asia: China, Japan and South Korea', Cambridge Judge Business School Working Paper, No. 10/2011, University of Cambridge.

Wells, K.M. (2015) *Outline of a Civilisation*, Leiden: Brill.

Witt, M.A. and Stahl, G.K. (2016) 'Foundations of responsible leadership: Asian versus Western executive responsibility orientations toward key stakeholders', *Journal of Business Ethics*, 136: 623–638.

World Bank (2016) *Republic of Korea*. www.worldbank.org/en/country/korea [accessed on 30 March 2017].

World Economic Forum (2016) *The Global Gender Gap Report 2016*. www.weforum. org/reports/the-global-gender-gap-report-2016 [accessed on 30 March 2017].

Yang, I. (2006) 'Jeong exchange and collective leadership in Korean organizations', *Asia Pacific Journal of Management*, 23: 283–298.

5 Business leaders and leadership in Taiwan

Introduction

Taiwan is one of the small but dynamic economies in the East Asian region, with a history of significant development in terms of economy and human talent. After 50 years of rapid economic growth, Taiwan has achieved a remarkable stage of development, as demonstrated in Table 5.1. Although Taiwan has a small economy and limited population, it achieved a GDP per capita of US$22,469 in 2015, with a very high level of disposable personal income. As a dynamic economy in East Asia, globally, Taiwan ranks fifteenth (out of 140) among the most competitive economies and fourteenth (out of 186) among the most attractive investment markets. It also has a relatively low ranking in terms of corruption. In recent years, Taiwan's inward foreign direct investment (FDI), mostly from mainland China, has been higher than its outward FDI, which has been historically very strong (see Zhu and Warner, 2001).

In recent years, Taiwan has shifted from traditional manufacturing and simple processing industries to a more advanced knowledge-based and service economy (Zhu and Warner, 2001; Zhu, 2003). Although there are many positive historical factors contributing to this development, the recent economic slowdown and political instability due to the 2016 change of government from the Nationalist Party (NP) to the Democratic Progress Party (DPP) may create significant uncertainties and instabilities, in particular with regard to economic ties with mainland China. Business leaders worry that the new government will not recognize the so-called '1992 Consensus' of a one China principle, causing the mainland government to terminate all engagement with Taiwan for the rest of the DPP's term in government. It should not be forgotten that the real drivers of economic development in Taiwan are not politicians but business leaders in general, and small and medium enterprises (SMEs) in particular.

This chapter aims to illustrate the key aspects of business leaders and leadership in Taiwan through a number of layers of investigation, including: a historical review of the cultural tradition and the impact on business leadership; Western influence on developing a modern concept and model of

Table 5.1 Economic, business and social indicators in Taiwan (2015–2016)

GDP in 2015 (US$ billion)	528	Disposable personal income in 2016 (TWD million)	7,932,300
GDP per capita in 2015 (US$)	22,469	Employed workforce in 2016	11,251,000
Global competitive score in 2015 (1–7)	5.3	Corruption index in 2015 (1–100)	62
Global competitive rank in 2015 (out of 140)	15	Corruption rank in 2015 (out of 175)	30
International ranking as attractive investment in 2015 (out of 186)	14	FDI inward stocks by Jan. 2016 (US$ billion)	6.9
International ranking as most attractive investment in the Asia-Pacific region in 2015 (out of 20)	5	FDI outward stocks by Jan. 2016 (US$ million)	544

Source: Invest Taiwan 2016: http://investtaiwan.nat.gov.tw/eng/news_display.jsp?newsid=4229.

behaviour of business leadership; tension between conventional practices and new challenges to change; and the issue of leader development. Finally, the chapter concludes by evaluating the key aspects and highlighting a number of implications for literature and practice.

Traditional normative values on leadership

The traditional normative values in Taiwan share some of their roots with mainland China, namely the traditional philosophies of Confucianism, Daoism, Yijing, the Legalist School and later Buddhism. To some degree, the Chinese and Taiwanese management systems in general, and HRM/business leadership systems in particular, were influenced by traditional Chinese Confucian culture and values. Some of the key characteristics of these systems emphasized hierarchy, paternalism, strong personal loyalty and commitment, a mid-way (*zhongyong*) management philosophy, and the importance of face culture and *guanxi* networks in business and individual lives (Warner and Zhu, 2003; Warner, 2014; Ren and Zhu, 2015; Busse et al., 2016). The belief system (based on Confucianism) values harmony, the mid-way and the tendency to see individuals in a socially dependent context. However, historical impacts such as the political and military conflict between Communist-led mainland and Nationalist led Taiwan – as well as the historical influence of Japanese colonization and later American influence as major economic and investment players in Taiwan – have led management systems to become more complicated, with mixed and hybrid elements.

In particular, business leadership thought can be traced to its traditional philosophies, with the most prominent influence being Confucianism. Fundamentally, Confucianism emphasizes social order and hierarchy, as well as social relationships based on reciprocity (see Busse et al., 2016; Warner, 2016). Social order requires individuals in society to follow the 'three guides' and 'five principles' (namely *sangang wuchang*); social hierarchy divides people into categories with a sense of higher class (i.e. *shitaifu*), namely officials and intellectuals, and lower class (*shumin*), namely ordinary masses – including merchants and business people. The social order provides the rationale for individuals doing their own work well and with commitment, but the social hierarchy ensures that people obey the rules and follow the norms of social status. One way people can change their social status is to through education and passing official examinations in order to become ranked officials or officially recognized intellectuals as advisors to the ruling class. Based on these elements, people feel that being an official or intellectual brings glory to them and their families; and advancement through education is one important means of changing one's social status.

Given that the social order requires individuals to perform their work well with commitment, the spirit of the 'tinkerer' among businessmen, craftspeople, service workers and others is another important element of doing work well. The tinkerer has special characteristics, including strong commitment to work, paying attention to detail, being persistent in continuing improvement and working with sincerity and passion (People's Net, 2016). These qualities work together with reciprocal relationship building and can provide the foundation of productive social networks and economic relationships. In addition, by stressing the primacy of cohesion and stability by means of the creation of a social and political order through a mid-way of *zhong yong* (Warner, 2011), leaders in general (and business leaders in particular) can follow the principle of benevolence (*ren*) to advocate love for their subordinates, so that subordinates accept their place in the social hierarchy, engage in cooperative human harmony and have confidence in their leaders (Ren and Zhu, 2015). The modern-day style of such leadership behaviour helps build morality, nurtures work relationships, treats people with fairness and communicates effectively (Yu, 2011). Therefore, it seems that Confucius' ideas resemble elements of contemporary transformational leadership and value-based leadership (Smith et al., 2004). However, Confucianism does not perceive leaders as 'agents of change', as transformational leadership theorists do (see Rindova and Starbuck, 1997). Moreover, Confucianism combines charisma and morality by asserting that human nature is inherently good and that people can be swayed by the power of words. In more recent history, the influence of Confucianism on business leadership in Taiwan has been associated with the concept of paternalistic leadership combining benevolence, morality and authoritarianism (Lin et al., 2014; Zhu et al., 2007).

For many years, paternalistic leadership has been the dominating leadership style in Taiwan as a convention (Lin et al., 2014). This element is rooted in Confucius' spirit, as well as the influence of Japanese management concepts during the colonial period and the post-WWII economic construction period. Based on the current moral standards, there are both positive and negative elements comprising the principles and characteristics of paternalistic leadership. For example, being kind with *ren* character towards subordinates, taking care of the wellbeing of subordinates and setting a good example for followers can be seen as positive elements; but being a dominating, powerful figure with strong control over subordinates, adopting a top-down decision-making process and requiring absolute obedience from subordinates can be seen as very negative nowadays.

The underpinning philosophy of these actions reflects the traditional culture of paternalism and the 'rule of man' concept rooted in federalist society and related social hierarchy (Lin et al., 2014). However, in more recent history, a modified model of paternalistic leadership has emerged, with increasingly more positive elements and fewer negative elements. Hence, the combination of benevolence, morality and authoritarianism as a new model of such paternalistic leadership has a more profound influence on current daily management practices (Cheng et al., 2004). Further research on the consequent changes and the impact on effectiveness of this new model shows that business leaders who have more consideration for employees' wellbeing, show loyalty and trustworthy characteristics, are fair and keep their promises, and set a moral example positively affect employee satisfaction and commitment to their organization (Chen and Kao, 2009; Cheng et al., 2002; Jiang and Cheng, 2008; Wu et al., 2010). Therefore, we can see that even the conventional leadership style, with the influence of traditional culture and values, has been transformed and modified from time to time in order to fit into the contemporary political, economic, social and cultural environment. These changes are also not isolated from international influence, on which we will elaborate in the following section.

Influence of Western management practices

Since the 1960s, Taiwan has experienced many complex political and economic developments, with a strong Western (mainly US) influence (Zhu et al., 2000). On the economic development front, the different stages have been accompanied by different management patterns, with the introduction of Western management theories and concepts. In Taiwan, for instance, economic development since the 1960s can be divided into two stages: the 'export' expansion period between 1961 and 1980; and the 'technology-intensive industries' expansion period from 1981 to 1997 before the Asian Crisis (Lee, 2002; Zhu et al., 2000; Zhu and Warner, 2004). In more recent years, since 2000 there has been an emerging service-oriented economy (Chen and Wallace, 2011). Generally speaking, the changes in the economy and labour market, the challenges of the Asian Crisis and, more broadly, global economic competition have required a different leadership style among

Taiwanese enterprises. Many new and younger-generation business leaders have begun to consider a combination of conventional Chinese leadership styles and Western leadership concepts, such as charismatic leadership, transformational leadership, and ethical and virtue leadership (Uen et al., 2011; Yang et al., 2014; Yui and Tsai, 2014). It is important to understand the evolution of the transformation under the influence of Western leadership concepts; the following sections provide a detailed illustration.

Generally speaking, Western influence in Taiwan derived predominately from the US as provider of most of the political, economic and military support to the country during the Cold War in defence against the expansion of Communism in East Asia. Due to the many American-based multinational enterprises (MNEs) investing in Taiwan – as well as the introduction of American management concepts and practices at universities in Taiwan (see Warner, 2014: 161) – individuals newly trained and graduating from these MNEs and universities became very familiar with Western management concepts and practices, adopting them in their work environment in their roles as business leaders and employers.

Given the transformation of large Taiwanese family businesses from traditional family business operations to modern management practices – with changes in corporate governance, professional management teams and new organizational structures and culture – a hybrid organization appeared with a combination of characteristics (Smith and Wang, 1996). The conventional paternalistic leadership could no long cope with the reality of such a transformation. Therefore, a process of modification of paternalistic leadership was gradually carried out, with the introduction of charismatic leadership and transformational leadership under the influence of Western management practices.

Tensions

The word *charisma* has Greek roots meaning a divinely inspired gift from God. Weber (1947) pointed out that charisma indicates an influential power that differs from traditional formal power, and is rather subordinates' recognition of their leaders' special capabilities. A leader with special capabilities provides a vision that emphasizes reciprocity and meets the needs of social transformation (Strange and Mumford, 2002). Such a vision attracts followers who believe their leader is extraordinary, and who therefore follow the leader wholeheartedly (Trice and Beyer, 1986). Given the transformation of business environments, more and more leaders have adopted charismatic leadership combined with certain elements of paternalistic leadership, particularly on moral principles, reflecting elements of ethical leadership in the West. The research findings by Su and Huang (2006) show that the new combination model based on certain elements of charismatic leadership, paternalistic leadership and moral/ethical leadership has an incremental effect; such a leadership style is better received by subordinates and leads to greater satisfaction. Another interesting finding is that adopting only charismatic leadership is less effective compared with the combination model or the paternalistic leadership model. This reinforces the concept of contextual determination that attributes an important role to traditional values in the modern work environment (Antonakis et al., 2003). Pure Westernization would not work well in a different social/cultural environment.

Another Western leadership concept, namely *transformational leadership*, also plays a certain role in the process of reforming leadership in Taiwan. Transformational leadership can provide idealized influence, inspirational motivation, individualized consideration and intellectual stimulation to subordinates (Bass, 1990; Sivanathan et al., 2005). Some of these elements have similar characteristics to paternalistic leadership, such as idealized influence and individualized consideration; but it also brings some unique qualities beyond conventional leadership in Taiwan, such as inspirational motivation and intellectual stimulation. Empirically based research in Taiwan by Uen et al. (2011) shows that providing training to leaders in order to familiarize them with the concept of transformational leadership and giving them more opportunities to implement it in the workplace are the most significant steps for adopting transformational leadership. However, these steps are not enough. It is also important to ensure the quality of leaders by equipping them with strong organizational identity. The perception of organizational leader proto-typicality represents the subordinates' trust in leaders who will act on their behalf, based on the interests of the organization. Without a good example of leaders with organizational identity, subordinates could question whether their leaders are true transformational leaders. In this sense, consistent conventional paternalistic leadership emphasizing the role model of the leader adds value to the adoption of the Western concept of leadership in Taiwan.

In recent years, research has also focused on the relationship between the adoption of transformational leadership and employees' job satisfaction, organizational commitment and organizational citizenship behaviour (Yang et al., 2014). Results show that they all have a positive correlation, namely adopting transformational leadership has positive effects on all three factors.

Another area of consideration is the impact of ethical leadership in Taiwan. In fact, there are many commonalities between ethical leadership and conventional paternalistic leadership with the emphasis on moral principles and the good ethical role model of the leader. However, both forms of leadership have different orientations (Yu and Tsai, 2014). For example, although both concepts emphasize the moral example set by leaders to subordinates, ethical leadership pays more attention to the legal, binding elements and the 'rule of law', and paternalistic leadership focuses on individual leaders' own behaviour and the 'rule of man'. Under the modern management system, ethical leadership makes a complementary contribution to the traditional management practices in Taiwan by establishing adoptable rules and standards as norms that everyone can learn and follow. This would allow both leaders and employees to behave according to the rules and laws, and communicate on what behaviour is legal or illegal. The empirical research by Yu and Tsai demonstrates that ethical leadership has a positive impact on employees' job satisfaction, and consequently influences employees' work in terms of more positive and innovative behaviour.

The phenomena illustrated above demonstrate a unique combination of Eastern and Western management thinking and practices. Some of them have similar roots and others are complementary. These approaches reconfirm the importance of contextual factors in relation to the modification and adoption of different styles of leadership as well as a realistic selection process of suitable leadership, subject to particular political, economic and social/cultural norms.

In January 2016, one of the authors visited Taiwan and interviewed a number of business leaders running different kinds of businesses, including a new online IT company, a new media design company, a small family-owned trading company and a large national bank branch.[1] The overall impression from the interviews was that an overwhelming tension existed between different leadership styles, with Eastern and Western orientation being adopted among different business leaders. A number of key observations can be made with regard to these phenomena. For example, in more traditionally oriented organizations such as the family-owned company and the bank, traditional values still influence the daily management style, with a greater emphasis on relationship building and less (although still important) on task-oriented leadership. The underlying concept is that a better relationship between leader and subordinate will enable the work team to achieve better outcomes. However, in the case of the newly established IT company and media design company, younger-generation leaders tend to adopt more Western-oriented concepts, such as the role of the leader as mobilizer, integrator, symbolizer, auditor and ambassador. Young leaders believe that if they are to be effective leaders, they need to be prepared to adopt the concept of situational leadership in order to bring success and flexibility to their business. As adoptive leaders, they need to develop the habit of ongoing learning through self-development. Nowadays, most company leaders undertake online e-learning and obtain professional licences in order to maintain their leadership position. In addition, these leaders encourage their subordinates to take self-development initiatives through e-learning and set a good example for their subordinates to follow.

One of the significant impacts is related to different cultural influences resulting from the process of globalization. Most Taiwanese companies deal with suppliers, customers and competitors globally; they have to adopt new ways of thinking and acting by learning and implementing these new concepts comprising of different cultural elements in their workplace. Leadership is also about mentoring and training others. If leaders do not have these leadership capabilities, they cannot help others to improve. The leader at the media company mentioned that he adopted a mixed leadership style through ongoing learning, including the Japanese style (i.e. paying attention to detail), the American style (showing charisma) and the Chinese style (taking the midway and emphasizing reciprocity and *guanxi*). He mentioned that he created an atmosphere in the workplace where people treated each other more equally and he was just one of their colleagues. By doing so, the entire team worked very well as a family where 'brothers and sisters' supported each other. This case demonstrates how a combination of leadership styles is implemented, albeit still in a fundamentally Chinese cultural environment.

Another common element found is the concept of self-sacrifice as part of the experience of being a business leader. Given the uncertain business environments both in Taiwan and globally, leaders have to spend extra time and energy dealing with many unexpected issues from time to time, requiring them to sacrifice their personal and family lives in order to handle these problems effectively.

Based on the phenomena illustrated above, we can see that the leadership styles among Taiwanese business leaders are mixed/hybrid, with different orientations according to the history and characteristics of the organization, as well as individual leaders' personal traits and capabilities.

Leader development

In Taiwan formal business leader development takes place through the management education systems. Highly trained business leaders have increasingly become *de rigueur* as companies seek to keep up with their rivals and enhance their competitive advantage. A new kind of international manager/leader is currently needed, one able to manage at home as well as abroad, and equipped with foreign languages and knowledge of foreign markets and workforces. As investment in management education and training is only one of several variables in promoting both micro- and macroeconomic performance, it is difficult to evaluate the distinct contribution of this investment. The number of trained managers/business leaders, especially at the top levels, is relatively limited vis-à-vis the aggregate size of the labour force.

It is evident that management education and training in Taiwan has followed the North American model (Zhu and Warner, 2013; Warner, 2014). Taiwan developed US-style business schools in the post-war period and has adapted them to its needs At the same time, traditional values based on Confucianism still influence the education system and its development (Smith, 1991; Yu, 2011). Taiwan has sought international recognition for its business schools; 27 business schools have obtained accreditation from the Association to Advance Collegiate Schools of Business (AACSB, 2011). Generally speaking, management education and training in Taiwan covers both undergraduate and postgraduate programmes, including full-time and part-time MBAs, EMBAs and online courses. Self-learning is another important method of obtaining knowledge given that online courses and other social media provide multiple channels for business leaders to learn and develop through self-initiative, as was clearly seen in the interviews conducted.

Since the management system was substantially influenced by the Japanese system, the internal labour market for selecting leaders in the workplace, including supervisors and managers, dominates the promotion system among Taiwanese firms. Similar to the situation in Japan, the majority of lower-level supervisors enter the enterprise directly from secondary school or vocational college. After on- and off-the-job training and rotation through different jobs and positions, recruits may be selected as supervisors and team leaders. The major tasks for their skill improvement relate to leadership qualities, communication, quality control and productivity enhancement. Most of them may stay in supervisor level positions, but some may be promoted to middle-management positions, with extra training focused on developing competency in the areas of professional, interpersonal, administrative and mental skills (Hong et al., 1996).

Beyond this level, other business leaders, including senior and middle managers, are more likely to be selected from recruits who entered the company with higher qualifications, such as a university degree or MBA, as well as many years of business experience. Some may be recruited directly from the labour market as experienced managers previously working in other companies. Higher-level graduates have to demonstrate their ability and talent for the first few years in order to gain promotion. Further training, in particular in multi-skilling, is necessary for management selection. As Chen and Wallace (2011) claimed, multi-skilling training enables business leaders to achieve high-quality performance and improves the overall satisfaction level among both managers and employees. Leaders recruited directly from the labour market normally have accumulated sufficient experience and, except for orientation training to familiarize them with the new organizational system, no further training is provided unless individuals have a particular need. Fang et al. (2010) indicated some crucial elements for developing competency among leaders in the healthcare industry, which include managerial competency, planning competency, interpersonal competency, professional/technical competency and personality. The survey results of the abovementioned study identified the three most important competencies among Taiwanese business leaders. The most important competency is related to personality. Some leaders may have unique traits, such as the ability to manage and be proactive. Planning ability is the second important characteristic, namely the ability to plan, organize, lead and control. The third important competency is professional/technical competency, which requires leaders to have knowledge of their particular professional areas (Fang et al., 2010).

Most senior business leaders have to undergo further training and development. Rotation of management positions and on-the-job training in senior leader mentoring programmes are common practice, but some key positions need higher levels of formal training, either within Taiwan or overseas, for training at prestigious institutions or to manage offshore subsidiaries. A national vocational training survey indicated that the proportion of manager training occurring within firms, training institutes and abroad was 54 per cent,

43 per cent and 3 per cent respectively (San, 1990). Nowadays, given that a large number of Taiwanese businesses are operating in mainland China, many middle and senior managers are sent to China to manage these businesses, with the prospect of promotion to higher positions after a number of years.

Lin (1998: 8) indicated that some particular skills and managerial competencies were needed for senior business leaders in Taiwan, including management skills, market sensitivity, resource creation and utilization, and technical skills. Examples include effective leadership, employee-centred practices and the establishment of appropriate organizational culture. According to a recent report by Development Dimensions International, more Taiwanese companies increased their leadership development budgets in 2011 compared to organizations globally, and more of them planned to continue that practice in 2012. The most critical skills for senior leadership in Taiwan include executing organizational strategy, driving and managing change, and building customer satisfaction and loyalty. Regarding the skills Taiwanese leaders are going to need most in the future, managing organizational talent was identified by most Taiwanese business leaders as critical (DDI 2011: 9–11). There is a strong indication that Taiwanese companies are taking a more proactive, long-term perspective on their businesses. The following aspects were claimed as the top three future skills according to the report, namely driving and managing change, fostering creativity and innovation, and identifying and developing future talent (DDI, 2011: 11).

Evaluation and conclusion

Under the influence of globalization, there is overwhelming tension between different leadership styles, with both Eastern and Western orientations being adopted by different business leaders in Taiwan. From the illustration above based on the literature and fieldwork interviews, we can see that the leadership styles among Taiwanese business leaders are mixed/hybrid, with different orientation according to the history and characteristics of the organization, as well as individual leaders' personal traits and capabilities. The evidence shows that merely adopting Western leadership concepts and practices is likely to be less effective than combining them with positive elements of conventional Eastern leadership styles.

It is clear that Taiwan has made great progress in the area of global business engagement, and provides strong support for both business leaders and employees to improve their global knowledge and multicultural business leadership capabilities through education, training and self-development. We must note that under the transformation, Confucian traditional values have had a very strong influence on today's businesses. Organizational initiate leadership/HR development and higher education programmes are also closely linked to the economic needs of society, which helps develop a 'cohesive society' as part of the nation-building policy. As the competitive forces of globalization grow, the development of business leadership in Taiwan will arguably increasingly be in the direction of providing capable business leaders not only working in Taiwan, but also in the Asia Pacific region and throughout the world. Taiwan is certainly in a strong position to develop such capabilities in order to strengthen its international competitiveness, cross-border political realities permitting.

Note

1 Zhu interviewed a number of business leaders in Taipei.

References

AACSB (2011) *Association to Advance Collegiate Schools of Business: Data Trends.* www.aacsb.edu/publications/businesseducation/2011-data-trends.pdf [accessed on 11 July 2016].

Antonakis, J., Avolio, B.J. and Sivasubramaniam, N. (2003) 'Context and leadership: An examination of the nine full-range leadership theory using the multifactor leadership questionnaire', *Leadership Quarterly*, 14(3): 261–295.

Bass, B.M. (1990) *Bass & Stogdill's Handbook of Leadership: Theory, Research and Managerial Implications*, New York: Free Press.

Busse, R., Warner, M. and Zhao, S. (2016) 'In search of the roots of HRM in the Chinese workplace', *Chinese Management Studies*, 10(3): 527–543.

Chen, H.Y. and Kao, H.S.R. (2009) 'Chinese paternalistic leadership and non-Chinese subordinates psychological health', *International Journal of Human Resource Management*, 20(12): 2533–2546.

Chen, L.C. and Wallace, M. (2011) 'Multiskilling of frontline managers in the five star hotel industry in Taiwan', *Research and Practice in Human Resource Management*, 19(1): 25–37.

Cheng, B.S., Xie, P.L. and Chou, L.F. (2002) 'School principles' leadership style, Quality of leader and subordinate relationship and teachers' behaviour: The effect of transformational and paternalistic leaderships', *Indigenous Psychological Research*, 17: 105–161.

Cheng, B.S., Chou, L.F., Wu, T.Y., Huang, M.P. and Farh, J.L. (2004) 'Paternalistic leadership and subordinate responses: Establishing a leadership model in Chinese organizations', *Asian Journal of Social Psychology*, 7: 89–117.

DDI (2011) *Taiwan Highlights: Global Leadership Forecast 2011*, Pittsburgh, PA: Development Dimensions International.

Fang, C.H., Chang, S.T. and Chen, G.L. (2010) 'Competency development among Taiwanese healthcare middle manager: a test of the AHP approach', *African Journal of Business Management*, 4(13): 2845–2855.

Hong, J.C., Wu, J.C. and Wu, M.H. (1996) 'Supervisor skill formation in Taiwan's automated factories', *Work Study*, 45(2): 22–26.

Jiang, D.Y. and Cheng, B.S. (2008) 'Affect- and role-based loyalty to supervisors in Chinese organizations', *Asian Journal of Social Psychology*, 11(3): 214–221.

Lee, J.S. (2002) 'Human resource development and Taiwan's move towards a knowledge-based economy', paper presented at HRD Task Force Symposium, Yunlin, Taiwan, 15–17 October.

Lin, C.Y.Y. (1998) 'Success factors of small- and medium-sized enterprises in Taiwan: An analysis of cases', *Journal of Small Business Management*, 36(4): 43–56.

Lin, T.T., Cheng, B.S. and Chou, L.F. (2014) 'Paternalistic leadership: Review and forecast', *Indigenous Psychological Research*, 42: 3–82.

People's Net (2016) 'Made in China requires the spirit of tinkerer', http://news.btime.com/news/20160428/n104862.shtml [accessed on 20 July 2016].

Ren, S. and Zhu, Y. (2015) 'Making sense of business leadership vis-à-vis China's reform and transition', *Leadership & Organization Development Journal*, 36(7): 867–884.

Rindova, V.P. and Starbuck, W.H. (1997) 'Ancient Chinese theories of control', *Journal of Management Inquiry*, 6(2): 144–159.

San, G. (1990) 'Enterprise training in Taiwan: results from the vocational training needs survey', *Economics of Education Review*, 9(4): 411–418.

Sivanathan, N., Turner, N. and Barling, J. (2005) 'Effects of transformational leadership training on employee safety performance: A quasi-experiment study', paper presented at the Academy of Management Meetings, Honolulu.

Smith, B.N., Montagno, R.V. and Kuzmenko, T.N. (2004). 'Transformational and servant leadership: Content and contextual comparisons', *Journal of Leadership and Organizational Studies*, 10(4): 80–91.

Smith, D.C. (1991) *The Confucian Continuum: Educational Modernization in Taiwan*, New York: Praeger.

Smith, P.B. and Wang, Z.M. (1996) 'Chinese leadership and organizational structures', in M. H. Bond (ed.), *The Handbook of Chinese Psychology*, Oxford and New York: Oxford University Press, pp. 322–327.

Strange, J.M. and Mumford, M.D. (2002) 'The origins of vision: Charismatic and ideological leadership', *Leadership Quarterly*, 13: 343–377.

Su, Y.F. and Huang, J. (2006) 'Charismatic, paternalistic and virtue leadership and follower effects', *Sun Yat-Sen University Management Review*: 14(4): 939–968.

Trice, H.M. and Beyer, J.M. (1986) 'Charisma and its routinization in two social movement organizations', *Research in Organizational Behaviors*, 8: 113–164.

Uen, J.F., Lin, C.S. and Chien, M.S. (2011) 'The relationship between transformational leadership and organizational identification: Moderating effect of perception of leader organizational prototypicality', *NTU Management Review*, 21(2): 265–285.

Warner, M. (2011) 'Society and HRM in China', *International Journal of Human Resource Management*, 22(16): 3223–3244.

Warner, M. (2014) *Understanding Management in China: Past, Present and Future*, London: Routledge.

Warner, M. (2016) 'Whither 'Confucian management?'', *Frontiers of Philosophy in China*, 11: 608–632.

Warner, M. and Zhu, Y. (2003) 'Human resource management "with Chinese characteristics": A comparative study of the People's Republic of China and Taiwan', in M. Warner (ed.), *The Future of Chinese Management*, London: Frank Cass, pp. 21–42.

Weber, M. (1947) *The Theory of Social and Economic Organizations*, New York: Free Press.

Wu, J.B., Tsui, A.S. and Kinicki, A.J. (2010) 'Consequences of differentiated leadership in groups', *Academy of Management Journal*, 53(1): 90–106.

Yang, M.L., Gong, R.W. and Chen, S.Y. (2014) 'A study of relationships between the transformational leadership and leadership performance: Perspectives of business leaders from mainland China and Taiwan', *Journal of Cheng Shiu University*, 27: 95–108.

Yu, J. (2011) 'The Confucian legacy and its implications for physical education in Taiwan', *European Physical Education Review*, 17: 219–230.

Yui, C.W. and Tsai, Y.L. (2014) 'A study of the relationships among ethical leadership and innovative work behaviors', *Journal of Humanities and Social Science*, 10(1): 59–66.

Zhu, Y. (2003) 'The post Asian financial crisis: Changes in HRM in Taiwanese enterprises', *Asia Pacific Business Review*, 9(4): 147–164.

Zhu, Y. and Warner, M. (2001) 'Taiwanese business strategies vis a vis the Asian financial crisis', *Asia Pacific Business Review*, 7(3): 139–156.

Zhu, Y. and Warner, M. (2004) 'HRM in East Asia', in A.W. Harzing and J. V. Ruysseveldt (eds), *International Human Resource Management* (2nd edition), London: Sage, pp. 195–220.

Zhu, Y. and Warner, M. (2013) 'Workforce development and skill formation in Taiwan: Social cohesion and nation building in a developmental state', in J. Benson, H. Gospel and Y. Zhu (eds), *Workforce Development and Skill Formation in Asia*, London and New York: Routledge, pp. 159–177.

Zhu, Y., Chen, I. and Warner, M. (2000) 'HRM in Taiwan: An empirical case study', *Human Resource Management Journal*, 10(4): 32–44.

Zhu, Y., Warner, M. and Rowley, C. (2007) 'Human resource management with Asian characteristics: A hybrid people management system in East Asia', *International Journal of Human Resource Management*, 18(5): 44–67.

6   Business leaders and leadership in Singapore

Introduction

The Republic of Singapore is located at the tip of the Malay Peninsula at the narrowest point of the Strait of Malacca, which is the shortest sea route between India and China. Once a British colonial trading post, today it is a thriving global financial hub and described as one of Asia's economic 'tigers' (Tulshyan, 2010). It is also renowned for its conservatism and strict local laws, and the country prides itself on its stability and security.

The history of Singapore began when the country became an independent republic, following an exit from Malaysia on 9 August 1965 when Lee Kuan Yew (2004–2011), a leader of the People's Action Party (PAP), declared Singapore a sovereign, democratic and independent state (LePoer, 1989). During Lee's term as Prime Minister from 1959 to 1990, his administration curbed unemployment, raised the standard of living and implemented a large-scale public housing programme. The country's economic infrastructure developed, racial tension was eliminated and an independent national defence system was created. Singapore evolved from a developing nation to first world status towards the end of the 20th Century. In 1990, Goh Chok Tong succeeded Lee as Prime Minister. During his tenure, the country tackled the economic impact of the 1997 Asian financial crisis and the 2003 SARS outbreak, as well as terrorist threats posed by the Jemaah Islamiah (JI) after the 11 September attacks and the Bali bombings. In 2004, Lee Hsien Loong, the eldest son of Lee Kuan Yew, became the third Prime Minister (Hiok, 1985).

Although Singapore billed itself as a free enterprise economy, the economic role of government was pervasive. As governing body for both the state and the city, the government was responsible for planning and budgeting for everything from international finance to rubbish collection. The government controlled, regulated and allocated land, labour and capital resources. It set or influenced many of the prices on which private investors based business calculations and investment decisions (Quah, 1985).

State intervention in the economy had a positive impact, not only on the profitability of private businesses but also on the general welfare of the population. Beyond the jobs created in the private and public sectors, the government provided subsidized housing, education and health and recreational services, as well as public transportation. The government also managed the bulk of savings for retirement through the Central Provident Fund and Post Office Savings Bank. It also decided annual wage increments, and set minimum fringe benefits in the public and private sectors. State responsibility for workers' welfare won the government the support of the population, thus guaranteeing political stability, which in turn encouraged private investment. In general, state intervention in the economy succeeded in being pro-business without being anti-labour, at least in matters regarding material welfare (LePoer, 1989).

Singapore's population is multi-ethnic, with a society made up of Chinese, Malay, Indonesian and Indian people, alongside many other minority groups. Its population is also multicultural, with 77.8 per cent of people being Chinese, 14 per cent Malay, 7.1 per cent Indian and the rest of the population consisting of Eurasians and other groups (Department of Statistics, 2016). Singapore has never had a dominant culture which immigrants could assimilate; nor has it had a common language. This was the foundation upon which the efforts of the government and ruling party to create a common Singaporean identity in the 1970s and 1980s rested (LePoer, 1989).

The 2015 Index of Economic Freedom ranks Singapore as the second freest economy in the world. It is the only Asian economy which has achieved triple-A status among the world's leading credit agencies. From the late 1990s, Singapore's economic growth rate has been among the highest in Asia. In 2015, it achieved a global competitive rank of two out of the 140 countries counted. Singapore's nominal GDP has reached US$292.7 billion, with a nominal GDP per capita of US$52,888, making it the highest in the Asia Pacific region (Table 6.1).

This chapter presents the key characteristics of business leaders and leadership in Singapore through a qualitative investigation using secondary data and in-depth interviews with relevant business leaders in two categories: multinational corporations (MNCs) operating in Singapore, and local small and medium-sized enterprises (SMEs). This chapter presents detailed findings of key themes such as historical and cultural tradition, and the impact on business leaders, foreign influence on developing modern practices of business leadership through their FDI in the country. It also discusses the tension between traditional practices and the new concepts that have been brought about by foreign businesses in recent years, as well as the development of leadership skills through training programmes by both formal and informal channels.

In examining these themes, this chapter is organized as follows: the next section analyses the Singaporean traditional values on leadership in order to provide an overview with regard to the impact of cultural contexts on Singaporean modern business leadership practices. This second section also outlines key elements of Chinese values and their historical influences on the country. This, in turn, provides a foundation for an analysis grounded in the

Table 6.1 Economic, business and social indicators in Singapore (2015–2016)

GDP in 2015 (US$ billion)	292.7	Disposable personal income in 2014/15 (US$)	105,537
GDP per capita in 2015 (US$)	52,888	Employed workforce in 2016	3,655,600
Global competitive score in 2015 (1–7)	5.68	Corruption index in 2015 (1–100)	85
Global competitive rank in 2015 (out of 140)	2	Corruption rank in 2015 (out of 175)	8
Global opportunity score in 2015 (1–10)	8.70	FDI inward stocks by the end of 2015 (S$ million)	23,377.2
Global opportunity rank in 2015 (out of 136)	1	FDI outward stocks by the end of 2015 (S$ billion)	665.4

Source: Global Opportunity Index 2015: www.globalopportunityindex.org/pdf/2015-Global-Opportunity-Index.p.

economic, social and cultural contexts relating to the mix-and-match of Western and Eastern leadership styles in modern Singapore. The third section explains the adoption of foreign practices in Singaporean companies, including a review of challenges faced by modern management and leadership. The fourth section will analyse the current tensions and challenges in the development of business leadership and the interventions of government in this regard. The fifth section will present key characteristics of leadership development programmes in modern Singapore. The chapter will then conclude with a general evaluation and suggestions for Singapore's future development in terms of business leadership.

Traditional normative values on leadership

Singapore's society appears to take account of collectivist social tendencies for compliance, and cultural tendencies for harmony and conflict avoidance that result in a general attitude of abidance and conflict avoidance (Hofstede, 1980; Redding, 1990; Hava and Kwok-bun, 2012). The country has been strongly influenced by Chinese cultural values, mixed with British culture and other cultures in Southeast Asia. Even though this colonial society was compartmented into ethnic and linguistic groups, Chinese cultural values have had a great influence over the culture and leadership styles adopted there. The Chinese have been a majority group in Singapore since 1830, but have themselves been divided into sometimes antagonistic segments speaking mutually unintelligible Chinese languages. Confucianism, we may note, has been emphasized by both community and government (Li et al., 2013). Leadership among the Chinese is also reflected in the role of clan associations. Nearly all of the traditional Chinese associations have been initiated, controlled and led by wealthy businesspeople with high social status and prestige as leaders. With this link to leadership, these associations have been turned into an institutional base for those who aspire to become dialect or community leaders. Over the years, a strong conviction in the association of leaders has developed amongst the Chinese – a leader is required to be public spirited, generous and willing to serve. An example of a successful clan association is the *Ngee Ann Kongsi*, which was founded in the 20th Century by 12 families who subsequently developed Ngee Ann City, Singapore's largest shopping mall, in a joint venture with a Japanese department store (Li et al., 2013).

Singapore's leadership style clearly derives from its Chinese traditional background. In this respect, it is similar to Hong Kong and Taiwan. The Confucian and Neo-Confucian legacy involves respect for authority, social relations – such as *guanxi* – and obligations to employees (see Redding, 1993). These are all part and parcel of what has been called Confucian dynamism. One writer in the field, Charles Rarick, makes a plausible case for 'Confucian Management', maintaining:

> Leadership under the Confucian tradition emphasizes a holistic concern for the welfare of employees, a concern for harmony in groups, team-work, and self-sacrifice. At the same time, Confucian leaders are frugal and demand loyalty and dedication to the organization. They expect employees to work tirelessly for the good of the group, the organization, and the nation. They tend to be autocratic and maintain tight control over the organization.
>
> (Rarick, 2007: p. 27)

The above-mentioned traits may well be regarded as the bed-rock of Singaporean managers. Singaporean business leadership is influenced by Confucian traditions such as strong hierarchy in organizations, where the elder's opinions always need to be listened to and respected. However, some divergent elements were found in this study, revealing that the characteristics of Singaporean business leaders are a unique case among Southeast Asian nations.

Chinese management in Singapore may be likened to Japanese management beliefs and practices of *oyabun*, or 'father' leadership (Hanada and Yoshikawa, 1991). The business leader is committed, as a father would be, to look after his staff's welfare; his staff member is committed and remains loyal to him. With mutual commitment and loyalty, the spirit of harmony is fostered, thus ensuring industrial peace. Both the manager and his staff behave like father and children in one happy family. Staff training, coaching and mentoring becomes critical. A participant in our study, a leader in an SME, argued that Singaporean companies differ from Western companies in their approaches to hiring and firing, since in Singapore the employer/management takes care of their employees in reciprocal relationships (Li et al., 2013).

Members of Singaporean companies display a particular sentiment or trait referred to as *kum cheng* (Hokkien dialect) or *ganqing* (Mandarin), which means a relationship based on a sense of mutual value of loyalty. Singaporean leaders show care and concern for their employees, who in turn are expected to feel concern and care for the company. Business leaders and managers prefer personal communication and coaching in their approach to employees, and take personal interest in their welfare. Businesses are run on the basis of good relationships; employees are treated like family members, and leaders view their enterprises as an extension or part of their traditional families. Informality and intimacy exist, with everyone undertaking a variety of activities to meet daily performance demands. Both leaders and employees are expected to be mutually reliable and trustworthy.

The majority of Singaporean indigenous firms are family businesses where leadership has passed through a few generations in the owner-families. The young leaders always consult their elders on their innovative ideas, and decisions are most likely to derive from advice given by the elders. This Paternalistic Leadership (Chao and Kao, 2005; Chen and Kao, 2009; Farh and Cheng, 2000) or Father Leadership (Cheng Low, 2005) is common practice in Asia, but has led to less flexibility in decision-making processes in Singapore. Such leadership combines authoritarianism, together with fatherly benevolence and moral integrity (Cheng et al., 2000). A paternalistic leader is said to be expected to act as a symbol equivalent to a 'parent' and treat employees as their children, particularly in Asia. In other words, traditional Singapore managers or leaders typically make decisions promptly and order their subordinates to take certain actions (without sufficiently explaining the rationale), expecting their subordinates to comply regardless of the correctness of those actions. Although these traditional Singaporean leaders show little respect for the opinions of their subordinates, they try hard to make all their employees feel that they are members of a large extended family. A local manager of an SME stated that he often visits his employees or their family members when they are ill, and often helps to pay some of their medical expenses if needed. By doing so, he makes his employees feel like they are part of the company's family. According to Hofstede (1980), such a paternalistic, autocratic leadership style tends to be favoured in all large Power Distance societies in Asia. Other researchers have tried to explain this observation in the context of Singapore. For instance, it has been argued that the large Power Distance in Singapore's culture could be attributed to the autocratic rule of British and Japanese governors before the independence of Singapore (Yeh, 1988). Following the influx of direct foreign investment into Singapore in the 1970s, more advanced management practices were gradually introduced. In particular, with American, Japanese, German, French and British MNCs being the major investors in Singapore, new cultural values and leadership styles were introduced to Singaporeans. These new styles and practices subsequently influenced the behaviours of local managers and leaders (Li et al., 2013).

Several studies have demonstrated the changes in leadership style in Singapore over recent years. For example, a study by Koh and Hia (1997) found that the interactive leadership style commonly practised in the Singaporean banking industry has two major components: female interaction skills and team-building orientation in management. The female interactive leadership is not limited to women. This is especially true in Oriental societies where the cultural value of collectivism is dominant (Koh and Hia, 1997). These skills include such elements as being a good listener, showing empathy, sharing information with others and a 'soft' approach in dealing with people (Stanford et al., 1995). A team-building orientation is also considered an important characteristic of interactive female leadership (Rosener, 1990; Stanford et al., 1995). This style of leadership includes fostering mutual trust and respect among people, and involving them in team building, which are the consistent elements of a transformational leadership approach.

Findings from a GLOBE study on leadership styles in Singapore show the key characteristics and 'Qualities of a Capable Leader' included being hardworking, knowing how to identify and capitalize on opportunities, and overcoming great difficulties to achieve great success in business. The participants in this study, in turn, valued the critical quality of a leader as 'the ability to get things done'. An important finding from this study was that even though Confucianism is the principal philosophy in Singaporean leadership (as discussed above), regarding morality as a key element in good leadership, participants did not mention Confucianism in the list of Qualities of a Capable Leader (Li et al., 2013).

Singaporean social values are distinct from other Chinese-based societies, including mainland China, in certain aspects. For example, traditional Chinese culture is strongly based on the philosophy of Confucius, which emphasized the importance of farming rather than business. Business people were considered to be the lowest in the social hierarchy, below officials, intellectuals, farmers and craftsmen. Values in Singapore, however, emphasize entrepreneurial spirit and encourage the setting up of businesses, especially family-run businesses (Hicks, 1993). These differences can be explained by studying the history of the early ethnic Chinese settlers who came to Singapore as traders, some of them being brought into Singapore in the 19th Century as indentured labour. Many of these labourers later set up their own businesses. With the development of the Malay Peninsula as a major tin- and rubber-producing region at the beginning of the 20th Century, a major business activity of these Chinese people became that of purchasing goods from Malaysia and Indonesia, and then selling them to European or American importers. An outcome of this trading activity was the development of the 'traders' mentality', which is acknowledged to still persist in Singapore society today (Cheong, 1991).

Another key element influencing managerial leadership in Singapore is the educational background of the country's first-generation political leaders, who came from the British-educated Peranakan elite (including the country's most influential leader, Lee Kuan Yew, ex-Deputy Prime Minister Goh Keng Swee and ex-Cabinet Minister Lim Kim San). Along with the British during the colonial period, these first-generation leaders formed many of the institutions that made Singapore what it is today. These leaders built a British-style public administration rather than a traditional Chinese structure as in its neighbouring economies of Hong Kong or Taiwan (Li et al., 2013). This heritage has had a strong influence on the formation of the country's culture and leadership style. As discussed earlier, business leadership in Singapore involves the heavy influence of the government in the economy and other aspects of social life (Cheng Low, 2005). Although Singapore inherited the same British model of governance as other Commonwealth states, its governing system has become widely known for efficiency and competence, especially in terms of its role in generating an 'economic miracle' which has resulted in the country transforming from a developing economy to one of the world's fastest-growing economies (Menon, 2007). The Singaporean governance system has been consistently rated by Transparency International as one of the most politically transparent and least corrupt in the world, but it is also often criticized for excessive interference in social issues. This heavy government involvement makes Singapore different from other Chinese communities indicating similar economic development, such as Hong Kong and Taiwan. For instance, only in Singapore can one see such powerful government organizations such as the Economic Development Board (EDB) and the Trade Development Board (TDB). The government has either direct or indirect control over all the major local banks (Hiok, 1985). For example, the largest local bank, the Development Bank of Singapore (DBS), is well known for its government links. The Singaporean government often becomes involved in the mergers of local companies, including taxi companies, high-tech firms and banks. Consequently, the Singaporean economy is now dominated by two groups of large companies: the MNCs, of which there are some 7,000 in the country; and the government-linked companies (GLCs), which have penetrated almost all industries in Singapore, from taxi operations to newspaper publishers.

The GLCs have led the way in business trends, much to the consternation of many employees and officials within the PAP-affiliated National Trades Union Congress (NTUC). The government has pushed ahead with its agenda to link wage levels more directly to productivity and market forces, and recognizes the tripartite model of the industrial relations system which has been promoted by the International Labour Organization (ILO). Government, NTUC and businesses collaborate strongly in dealing with any employment issues. The government recognizes the nature of the process, and the NTUC calls for a new contract between employers and employees to ensure that these issues are successfully managed. It is argued that employers need to accept greater responsibility for boosting employee skill levels to cope with the changing economy, in return for which workers must accept wage flexibility and productivity-based measures (Rodan, 2005). This institutional environment also influences the behaviour of business leaders in terms of their interaction with their employees.

In 2006, the Singapore Human Resources Institute commissioned two visionary Human Resources Management (HRM) surveys at an organizational level to determine the views of employees as to 'what makes a good leader' (Choo, 2007). The key findings of these surveys demonstrated that there were substantial perceived gaps in leadership skills, such as motivating and inspiring, giving recognition for achievement and providing feedback. More positive findings emerged in leaders' relationships with staff, the quality of leadership performance and associated competencies. These important findings were discussed from the standpoint of engagement/recruitment as well as the strategies for human resource development, which are vital elements of healthy HRM policies and practices (Choo, 2007).

Influence of foreign management practices

The foreign direct investment (FDI) contribution to Singaporean economic development and the strong presence of foreign firms in the country's economy are key factors in Singaporean management practices. Since the country was established, the government encouraged FDI into the country by issuing many favourable policies. For example, tax incentives to encourage FDI were introduced in 1967 and extended later. This encouragement of foreign investment, particularly of MNCs, enabled Singapore to combine local productive factors with foreign technical and managerial know-how, and to overcome local producers' lack of knowledge or information about world markets. Over the years, the presence of foreign companies in the Singaporean economy has steadily increased. This is especially true in manufacturing in the 1980s, when foreign firms regularly accounted for more than 80 per cent of net investment. By 1984, for instance, foreign companies (defined as firms with more than 50 per cent foreign equity) produced 71 per cent of Singapore's total output, and accounted for 63 per cent of value added and 82 per cent of manufactured exports (Koh, 1987). The success of the US MNCs encouraged Japanese industrialists to move their middle technology factories to Singapore, and in the 1970s British companies which had withdrawn when their forces left the city-state returned to set up high-value-adding pharmaceutical operations. Singapore's rise as a financial centre was evident in the 1990s, by which time it had become the fourth-largest financial centre in the world after London, New York and Tokyo.

Singapore has acquired a wide selection of advanced management systems, developed and tested in different parts of the world. Most MNCs that operate in Singapore come from Organisation of Economic Co-operation and Development (OECD) countries. These businesses have had a major effect on the country's leadership style. In particular, Singaporean leadership style has been largely inherited from the British and, later, American styles in terms of Western management practices. The British influence came from the colonial administration as well as from British firms which were initially established in Singapore. Both of these streams played a role in introducing Western management theories and practices. American management systems and Japanese corporate philosophies have also been effectively implemented in the Singapore context (Torrington and Tan, 1998).

As part of its strategy for economic restructuring, the government encouraged local employers in the 1980s to adopt Japanese-style management practices to improve employee work attitudes, labour turnover, productivity and labour–management relations. The government held the belief that the Japanese 'role model' was culturally compatible with Singapore's values and aspirations because Singapore is culturally predominantly 'Chinese', and the Chinese and Japanese cultures have much in common. There are a number of differences between the extent to which the Japanese model was practised and the extent to which it was preferentially transferred into the Singaporean context. Some Japanese practices were widely adopted, such as consensual decision-making, but lifetime employment and seniority systems were not positively received. Japanese practices were found in the public (government) sector, but many businesses did not share the government's view (Gill and Wong, 1998).

A study by Gill and Wong (1998) of 32 companies in Singapore on five main practices associated with the Japanese style of management – including lifetime employment, seniority systems, house unions, consensual decision-making and quality (control) circles – suggested that house unions, consensual decision-making and quality circles were transferable to Singapore, but that lifetime employment and seniority systems were problematic for cultural reasons. These two key practices in the Japanese HRM model were unlikely to transfer successfully to Singapore. They argued that unlike Japan, organizations in Singapore had to earn employees' loyalty and commitment, and not take them for granted.

Results from another study by Fukuda (1988) of 43 Japanese subsidiaries operating in Singapore also show a similar result. This study found that there was a great deal of uncertainty among case studies about how well their practices transferred to Singaporean units. Japanese firms in general appeared to have a lower propensity to adopt their home practices in Singapore than other firms (e.g. American firms).

According to a Singaporean manager from a US MNC, the great impact of the US leadership style on the Singaporean workforce came even before the Japanese, in the early 1960s, when the first few US firms started to operate in Singapore – including Hewlett-Packard (HP), followed by General Electric, which set up six different facilities and by 1970 had become the largest single employer in Singapore (Zhang, 1994). By the 1980s the country had become a major electronics exporter, and by 1997 there were nearly 200 US manufacturing companies with over S$19bn worth of investments. In terms of knowledge transfer, American subsidiaries in Singapore usually prepare a long-term plan (three to five years) for their expatriates, providing for enough time to work with and train their local staff. The manager from the above-mentioned MNC stated that her company hired Singaporean managers for all levels of managerial, technical and supervisory personnel. This particular Singapore subsidiary gives local managers sufficient training and business exposure so that they can assume very senior management positions. The CEOs of her company are local employees, trained and promoted from within the organization. In general, the manpower management policies in a typical American subsidiary in Singapore are fairly well structured. Human resources management techniques such as job evaluations, promotion criteria for managerial and technical personnel, and training programmes are frequently employed. The training grants provided by the government-administered Skills Development Fund (SDF) have enabled the American companies to have long-term training programmes for the development of their employees.

While managers in US firms have strongly focused on adapting training and development policies into their Singapore subsidiaries, a manager of a Japanese MNC said that his company has promoted the value of teamwork or Japanese-style collectivism by setting up quality circles (QCs), because they believe QCs have improved teamwork both among workers and between workers and management. The activities of QCs also help increase employee morale and change the leadership style in Singapore from autocratic to more participative. Moreover, the subsidiaries of Japanese MNCs also encourage a leadership style that helps promote harmonious labour–management relations. This style is often characterized by management spending more time with the local staff, especially after office hours, through company dinners or after-dinner visits to bars and pubs.

Tension

There is a tension between exogenous influences and indigenous ones. Singapore welcomes FDI as well as foreign practices and ideas; but, at the same time, a wave of support for modification of foreign practices to adapt them to 'Singaporean characteristics' is strong among Singapore's leaders. It would be naive to say that all Western values are well received by this nation. There is a movement by the government to urge young Singaporeans to turn away from Western materialism and Western-style democracy, which are closely related to Western individualism (Chhokar et al., 2013). Findings from the GLOBE studies on societal cultural practices, values and leadership style in Singapore show that the Singaporean government has been instrumental in cultivating a greater degree of collectivism. This trend runs counter to other Chinese culturally based economies, including Hong Kong and Taiwan, which appear to have moved towards Western individualism in recent years (McGrath et al., 1992; Yeh and Lawrence, 1995). At the same time, many Western-educated Singapore professionals have emigrated to the West, including many middle managers who are also young professionals and received their education in the West in recent years. These young and well-educated employees often hold important positions in organizations, and are seen as the next generation of business leaders who seem to prefer less collectivism in their leadership style.

Findings from interviews show that Singaporean companies are well protected by the government and less flexible in self-directed activities in terms of overseas investment. The political stability has attracted FDI into the country in the last few decades to help develop a fast-growing economy. One participant in our study (a manager of a local company) argued that the stable government helps encourage FDI into the country but has negative effects on indigenous firms in terms of encouraging them to invest outside Singapore. Singaporean companies differ from foreign companies in that the government is their role model, leading the way in, for instance, overseas investments and ventures. The government not only maintains a heavy economic presence, but also makes individuals in the country much more dependent on the government, compared to countries such as Hong Kong. For example, the people in Singapore depend on the government for housing, low-cost medical services and pensions. One direct consequence of this heavy government involvement is an increase in 'uncertainty avoidance', a cultural value first identified by Hofstede (1980). This dependent relationship with the government has become so significant that, in recent years, even the Singaporean government leaders have begun to worry. Recently, a senior government official referred to Singaporeans as 'flowers in a greenhouse', unable to survive without the greenhouse (Li et al., 2013). An SME leader who participated in our study confirmed the view that Singaporean firms remain reluctant to venture abroad, disagreeing with the government's suggestions of safety for their business investments, because they think their companies are not sufficiently well developed to compete abroad compared to those from the developed economies of Hong Kong or Taiwan. Our participant claimed that Singaporeans are generally risk averse, preferring to take safe professional and managerial jobs rather than strike out on their own. While the government seeks to encourage Singapore companies to venture abroad, the local leaders believe they need to depend on their home-grown enterprises to develop entrepreneurs to lead the way.

Findings from the GLOBE study also show that Singaporean firms conducting business in foreign markets tend to adopt a different approach to their Hong Kong and Taiwanese counterparts. In China, for example, where firms from Hong Kong and Taiwan rely mainly on their kinship and friendship networks in China, the majority of Singapore firms rely on the networks built by the government. In other words, regardless of business opportunities, Singaporean investors prefer to invest in Chinese cities where their government has already established relations with the local governments. This approach thus favours lower risks (Chhokar et al., 2013).

The increasing role of women in leadership positions in Singapore has become another source of tension in recent year. The country is an affluent, developed country; human development and accessibility to resources are not viewed as obstacles to women's access to power. Even though this country has transformed itself from third world to a leading economy in the region within a generation, the number of women in leadership positions is much lower than in many other economies such as China and Vietnam. Since the introduction of an ethnic quota policy in 1988, minority ethnic groups already constitute 19 per cent of the Parliament; in contrast, women received no legal provisions, despite occupying less than 5 per cent of seats in the Parliament (Tan, 2014). With a lack of policy from government to promote women to leadership positions, Singaporean women still are struggling to break through a glass ceiling to further their careers. Singapore labour statistics show that while women make up nearly 45 per cent of the resident workforce, and have a literacy rate as high as 94.4 per cent, only 7.3 per cent of them take up directorships on the boards of companies (Statistics Singapore, 2012). In fact, an online survey has found that 74 out of 100 women surveyed from medium and large companies have turned down jobs due to work–life balance concerns (Lee, 2013). The lack of women in senior management and political positions shows that Singaporean women have not overcome all the socio-economic or institutional barriers to working in higher positions and political participation. To explain the cause behind such low involvement of women, an interviewee from a government office argued that issues of family, work and childcare that traditionally preoccupy women are still largely key issues. She argued that government support through action and policy promoting women would help change social norms. Supporting women with better childcare options and effective family–work life balance would be a way of addressing the under-representation of women at higher leadership levels.

Leadership development programmes in Singapore

In order to compete effectively in today's globalized knowledge economy, countries have to meet the increasing demand for highly skilled and knowledgeable leaders (Ng et al., 2015). To meet this demand, countries like Singapore have embarked on extensive educational reform to improve the performance of their students and future leaders (Barber and Mourshed, 2017). According to a participant in our study, who is an HR consultant for a government programme named 'Skill Future', business leaders in Singapore have faced great challenges in recent years to sustain their entrepreneurial spirit, because economic success in Singapore in the last few decades has brought about even higher expectations of success in businesses. However, the expectation of assured progress and growth exists alongside a reluctance to risk what Singaporean businesses already have. Our participant also stated that there appears to be a common perception among younger-generation Singaporeans that to be successful one need only do well at school, graduate with a good degree or diploma, and then join a large local or foreign company to have easy access the escalator of stable jobs, ever-growing wages and good future prospects.

This attitude has arisen from the country's educational background. No one would deny that the key contributors to the success of Singapore today can be conceptualized in terms of a strong focus on education across macro (societal, cultural, economic-political), organizational (school and classroom) and family (parenting and socialization) levels (Dimmock and Tan, 2013). At the macro-societal level, the Singaporean government has established a meritocracy as the basic value determining societal organization in the Republic. Specifically, academic merit measured by examination achievement is the basis of socio-economic status and reward. As written earlier, the government maintains high degrees of control over and aligns education, economy and society through a powerful elite bureaucracy (Ho, 2003). Education policy is driven largely by economic instrumentalism – efficiency and effectiveness – rather than by political ideology (Dimmock and Tan, 2013). The government identifies Singapore as a meritocracy that pays attention to its technocratic orientation. This means that policy formulation in Singapore is undertaken by individuals with specialized skills obtained through advanced educational achievement, the minimum requirement being a university degree. Consequently, leaders' promotion and tenure are based on educational qualifications and performance (Menon, 2007).

Today, Singapore has a variety of leadership development channels, ranging from formal training at well-known institutions or government programmes to informal business training offered by organizations. In terms of content, leadership development programmes deliver both professional knowledge and soft skills. Due to a strong focus on education, it is no surprise that Singapore is home to some of the best formal leadership training and development programmes in the region. Its universities are some of the most well-regarded business schools, such as the National University of Singapore (NUS), rated one of the top in Asia, as well as stand-alone institutions such as the Singapore Management University (SMU) and an external campus of INSEAD (originally the European Institute of Business Administration). The NUS and INSEAD options are rated first and third in the region (see FindMBA, 2017). These two institutes are also the top business schools for MBA qualifications in the Asia Pacific region. Both schools are highly competitive and offer an academically rigorous MBA programme.

The National University of Singapore runs the NUS Business School, which is consistently rated as one of the top business schools in the Asia Pacific region and one of the leading business schools worldwide. The Forbes Ranking of International Two-Year MBA programmes ranks the NUS MBA seventh globally out of a total of 11 schools listed, while the Quacquarelli Symonds Global 200 MBA Rankings 2014/15 ranks the NUS MBA second in Asia. In *The Economist* 2016 Full-Time MBA rankings, the NUS Business School's MBA programme slipped 12 places to 99th worldwide (sixth in Asia). In the *Financial Times* (*FT*) 2016 Global MBA Rankings, the Business School slid one spot down to 32nd globally (second in Singapore). The NUS Business School offers double degree programmes at top universities across Asia,

Europe and North America. The following paragraphs outline the partner universities that offer these programmes in association with NUS Business School.

INSEAD has three campuses globally – in Europe (France), Asia (Singapore) and the Middle East (Abu Dhabi). The institute became a pioneer of international business education with the graduation of the first MBA class on the Fontainebleau campus in France in 1960. In 2016 INSEAD topped an annual global ranking of MBA programmes. In the latest (2016) *FT* MBA rankings INSEAD climbed three spots ahead of elite business schools such as Harvard (Yang, 2016). Its Singapore campus was established in 2000. The full-time MBA programme at INSEAD is built around 14 core courses, and connects students with a strong alumni network of 23,833 located all over the world.

Established in 2000, the Singapore Management University specializes in business and management studies. The university provides an American-style education modelled on the Wharton School of the University of Pennsylvania. SMU is ranked one of Asia's top universities, debuting in the 2015 *FT* EMBA ranking at number 10 in Asia and 36 worldwide, making it the highest-ranked new entrant in 2015. SMU's Masters in Applied Finance is ranked number two in Asia and 34 worldwide by the *FT* and its Masters in Wealth Management programme was ranked number two worldwide by the *FT* in 2015, with London Business School ranked number one.

The Singapore Institute of Management (SIM) was established in 1964 as a not-for-profit facility with three distinct educational units aimed at a specific market segment of learners. SIM University (UniSIM) is a private university, established in 2005, offering more than 50 undergraduate programmes in various disciplines, and receives government subsidies and access to government bursaries, tuition fee loans and study loans. SIM Global Education (SIM GE) offers more than 80 academic programmes, ranging from its own diploma and graduate diploma courses to Bachelor's and Master's programmes with universities from the United States, the United Kingdom and Australia. Attracting 20,000 full-time and part-time students and adult learners from over 40 countries, SIM Professional Development (SIM PD) offers many short executive training programmes for individual professionals. Over 13,000 professionals benefit annually from these programmes. SIM PD's customized in-company training programmes also help companies optimize organizational effectiveness in various fields of management and human resource development (see SIM, 2017).

The government does not want to miss out on an opportunity to develop skills and business leadership for the future economy. The very well-known 'SkillsFuture' is a national government programme aimed at providing Singaporeans with the opportunities to achieve their fullest potential in life and become business leaders, regardless of their starting point. The programme aims:

> to develop skills for the future and support productivity-led economic growth by advancing SkillsFuture through the development of an

integrated system of education, training, and career progression for all Singaporeans; driving industry transformation by overseeing implementation of plans for key clusters through skills development, innovation, productivity and internationalization strategies; and fostering a culture of innovation and lifelong learning in Singapore.

(SkillsFuture, 2017)

This initiative is governed by the tripartite Council for Skills, Innovation and Productivity (CSIP); is chaired by the Deputy Prime Minister and Coordinating Minister for Economic and Social Policies; and comprises members from government, industry, unions and educational and training institutions. These members represent different sectors and bring together a broad range of expertise. CSIP was established in 2016, and takes forward the efforts undertaken to date by the SkillsFuture Council and the National Productivity Council (NPC).

The British Council in Singapore is partnering with a global emotional intelligence network, Six Seconds, to extend the Professional Development Centre to provide training on emotional intelligence and leadership skills in the Asia Pacific. This programme has been well regarded at an international level. There are few options for development that are both scientifically sound and practical for Singaporean leaders. This organization believes that increasing emotional intelligence is linked to dramatic improvements in decision-making and influences on leadership in Singapore (British Council, 2014).

Leadership development for local managers has been pursued by MNCs in recent years. Although most multinational firms started their operations in Singapore using the traditional expatriate model, today local employees represent a large percentage of the workforce. Therefore, many MNCs rely on leadership programmes tailored to local talent development, and utilize various tools and strategies to identify and train high-potential employees. One such tool seeks to develop a culture and initiatives for enhancing potential local leaders' visibility at company executive level. This strategy, which is aimed at creating leadership 'academies' or formal workshops for high-potential employees, has proven to be prevalent in various leadership development models throughout Asia. These workshops are frequently cross-functional and conducted on an international basis. They are often led by executives and top management themselves, and serve to provide exposure to high-potential employees and deliver action-learning projects to select participants. MNCs that implement this tool in their local leadership development programmes benefit from retaining top talent and developing well-rounded individuals who have gained significant experience through these cross-functional workshops and projects. Without this strategy, companies face the challenge of promoting individuals without the necessary international exposure and skills, or searching for talent outside the company. Recognizing top talent from within and enhancing high-potential individuals' visibility and exposure to core company values assures MNCs that their subsequent leaders will be equipped with the necessary skills, knowledge and priorities to run the company's operations in the future (Dunnagan et al., 2013).

Evaluation and conclusion

In this chapter, we have discussed how leadership style in Singapore can be seen as a combination of traditional Chinese Confucian values and modern Western practices (Zhang, 1994). In other words, the Singaporean leadership approach is 'halfway' between traditional Asian and Western practices. To understand the leadership characteristics in this country, we need to consider the interactions of various environmental factors, especially the significant role of early Chinese settlement that contributed to make the distinctive norms, the role of MNCs in the country's economic development and the heavy involvement of the government in day-to-day economic activities as well as society. In a society heavily influenced by Confucian cultural values, the role of government in shaping and changing the societal and organizational elements, as well as its influences on decision-making at firm levels, is highly significant. This situation is very different from that in societies featuring Western-style democracy. In Singapore, the government often influences society and leadership practices through its policies much more directly than in other advanced economies (Li et al., 2002). Chinese culture has been observed to have a great impact on individual Singaporeans' perceptions and attitudes with regard to leadership. To add to this complexity, there is also evidence of the development of Western norms and values among the young generation of leaders.

The culture in Singapore seems to have changed dramatically over the years, making it inappropriate to label its societal culture as Chinese or Asian (Li et al, 2013). This finding is important for future research into management styles and business leadership. It suggests the need to deal with the issues of leadership and management within a more dynamic, more comprehensive approach, where a combination of external and internal factors should be treated very carefully. With comparable levels of economic and technological development in modern Asian countries, other antecedents, such as government policy, may play much more significant roles. Consequently, in examining the impact of traditional cultural values, interactions among these factors should be considered.

Our findings also have some practical implications for managers and leaders within international business. As results from this study have suggested, significant differences even among East Asian Chinese societies exist. Accordingly, managers or leaders of international businesses need to pay more attention to the differences in cultural values and the factors that have caused the partial changes. MNCs need to pay attention not only to basic cultural differences between their home country and the host country, but also to differences between different societies that share the same language, religion and ethnic traditions (e.g. Singapore compared to Hong Kong and

Taiwan). This is also true for ethnic Asian managers from an Asian society, such as Singapore. Even in the case of an ethnic Asian manager, it is still necessary to understand cultural changes that have taken place in other Chinese societies. Experience from one Chinese society may not be applicable to other Chinese societies. A successful business policy in Hong Kong may not work well in Singapore, and a successful manager who works well in Taiwan may not work well in China. Without an awareness of the differences caused by cultural change and the consequences that follow, MNCs will risk failure in any attempts to generate effective strategies in areas such as selection and training, marketing and promotion, and business investment.

References

Barber, M., and M. Mourshed (2017) *How the World's Best-performing School Systems Come Out on Top*, London: McKinsey & Company.

British Council (2014) 'British council supporting leadership excellence in Singapore and APAC by increasing emotional intelligence in business and education', *China Weekly News*, p. 136, http://search.proquest.com.ezpprod1.hul.harvard.edu/doc view/1537010704?accountid=11311 [accessed on 17 February 2017].

Chao, A.A. and Kao, S. R. (2005) 'Paternalistic leadership and subordinated stress in Taiwanese enterprises', *Research in Applied Psychology*, 27(1): 111–131.

Cheong, W.K. (1991) 'The style of managing in a multicultural society-Singapore', in J. M. Putti (ed.), *Management: Asian Context*, Singapore: McGraw-Hill, pp. 258–283.

Cheng, B.S., Chou, L.F. and Farh, J.L. (2000) 'A triad model of paternalistic leadership: The constructs and measurement', *Indigenous Psychological Research in Chinese Societies*, 14(1): 3–64.

Chen, H.Y. and Kao, H.S.R. (2009) 'Chinese paternalistic leadership and non-Chinese subordinates psychological health', *International Journal of Human Resource Management*, 20(12): 2533–2546.

Cheng Low, P.K. (2005) 'Father leadership: The Singapore case study', *Management Decision*, 4(1): 89–104.

Chhokar, J.E., Brodbeck, F.C. and House, R.J. (2013) *Culture and Leadership across the World: The GLOBE Book of In-Depth Studies of 25 Societies*, London: Routledge.

Choo, H.G. (2007) 'Leadership and the workforce in Singapore: Evaluations by the Singapore Human Resources Institute', *Research and Practice in Human Resource Management*, 15(2): 104–114.

Department of Statistics (2016) 'Census of Population 2000 Statistical Release 1: Demographic Characteristics, Ministry of Trade and Industry, Republic of Singapore', www.singstat.gov.sg/publications/publications-and-papers/cop2000/cop2000r1 [accessed on 10 January 2017].

Dimmock, C. and Tan, C.Y. (2013) 'Educational leadership in Singapore: Tight coupling, sustainability, scalability, and succession', *Journal of Educational Administration*, 51(3): 320–340.

Dunnagan, K., Maragakis, M., Schneiderjohn, N., Turner, C. and Vance, C. (2013) 'Meeting the global imperative of local leadership talent development in Hong Kong, Singapore, and India', *Global Business and Organizational Excellence*, 32(2): 52–60.

Farh, J.L. and Cheng, G.S. (2000) 'A cultural analysis of paternalistic leadership in Chinese organizations', in J.T. Li, A.S. Tsui and E. Welson (eds), *Management and Organizations in the Chinese Context*, London and New York: Macmillan, pp. 84–127.

FindMBA (2017) 'Asia 100 Most Popular Business Schools 2017', http://find-mba.com/most-popular/asia [accessed on 11 June 2017].

Fukuda, K.J. (1988) *Japanese-Style Management Transferred: The Experience of East Asia*. London: Routledge.

Gill, R. and Wong, A. (1998) 'The cross-cultural transfer of management practices: The case of Japanese human resource management practices in Singapore', *International Journal of Human Resource Management*, 9(1): 116–135.

Hanada, M. and Yoshikawa, A. (1991) 'Shop-floor approach to management in Japan', in J. Putti (ed.), *Management: Asian Context*, Singapore: McGraw-Hill, pp. 36–60.

Hava, D. and Kwok-bun, C. (2012) *Charismatic Leadership in Singapore: Three Extraordinary People*, London: Springer.

Hicks, G.L. (1993) *Overseas Chinese Remittances from South East Asia 1910–1940*, Singapore: Selected Books.

Hiok, L.B. (1985) 'Singapore in 1984: A time for reflection and a time for change', *Southeast Asian Affairs*, 1: 297–305.

Ho, K.L. (2003) *Shared Responsibilities, Unshared Power: The Politics of Policy-Making in Singapore*, Singapore: Eastern Universities Press.

Hofstede, G. (1980) *Culture's Consequences: International Differences in Work-Related Values*, Beverly Hills, CA: Sage.

Koh, A.T. (1987) 'Linkage and the international environment', in L.B. Krause, K.A. Fee and L.T. Yuan (eds), *The Singapore Economy Reconsidered*, Singapore: Institute for Southeast Asian Studies, pp. 318–343.

Koh, W.K.L. and Hia, H.S. (1997) 'The effects of interactive leadership on human resource management in Singapore's banking industry', *International Journal of Human Resource Management*, 8(5): 710–719.

Lee, D. (2013) 'Survey: 74% of women turn down jobs due to work–life balance', *Straits Times*, 4 March 2013, www.straitstimes.com/breaking-news/singapore/story/survey-74-women-turn-down-jobs-due-worklife-balance-concerns-20130304 [accessed on 9 January 2017].

LePoer, B.L. (1989) *Singapore: A Country Study*, Washington, DC: Library of Congress.

Li, J., Karakowsky, L. and Lam, K. (2002) 'East meets West: the case of Sino-Japanese and Sino-West Joint Ventures in China', *Journal of Management Studies*, 39(6): 841–863.

Li, J., Ngin, P. and Teo, A. (2013) 'Culture and leadership: Combination of the East and the West', in J.E. Chhokar, F.C. Brodbeck and R.J. House (eds), *Culture and Leadership across the World: The GLOBE Book of In-Depth Studies of 25 Societies*, London: Taylor & Francis, pp. 947–968.

McGrath, R.G., MacMillan, I.C., Yang, E.A. and Tsai, W.T. (1992) 'Does culture endure, or is it malleable? Issues for entrepreneurial economic development', *Journal of Business Venturing*, 7: 441–458.

Menon, S. (2007) 'Governance, leadership and economic growth in Singapore', MPRA Paper No. 4741, 28 August, http://mpra.ub.uni-muenchen.de/4741/ [accessed on 10 January 2017].

Ng, F.S.D., Nguyen, T.D., Wong, B. and Choy, W. (2015) 'Instructional leadership practices in Singapore', *School Leadership & Management*, 35(4): 388–407.

Quah, J.S.T. (1985) 'Singapore in 1984: Leadership transition in an election year', *Asian Survey*, 25(2): 220–231.

Rarick, C. (2007) 'Confucius on management: Understanding Chinese cultural values and managerial practices', *Journal of International Management Studies*, 2: 22–28.

Redding, G. (1993) *The Spirit of Chinese Capitalism*, Berlin: Walter de Gruyter.

Rodan, G. (2005) 'Singapore in 2004: Long-awaited leadership transition', *Asian Survey*, 45(10): 140–145.

Rosener, J.B. (1990) 'Ways women lead', *Harvard Business Review*, 68(6): 119–125.

SIM (2017) *Singapore Institute Management*, www.sim.edu.sg [accessed on 11 June 2017].

SkillsFuture (2017) 'About the Council for Skills, Innovation and Productivity', www.skillsfuture.sg/what-is-skillsfuture.html [accessed on 11 June 2017].

Stanford, J., Oates, B. and Flores, D. (1995) 'Women's leadership styles: A heuristic analysis', *Women in Management Review*, 10(2): 9–16.

Statistics Singapore (2012) 'Statistics: Key annual indicators', www.singstat.gov.sg/statistics/latest_data.html [accessed on 10 January 2017].

Tan, N. (2014) 'Ethnic quotas and unintended effects on women's political representation in Singapore', *International Political Science Review*, 35(1): 27–40.

Torrington, D. and Tan, C.H. (1998) *Human Resource Management for Southeast Asia and Hong Kong*, Upper Saddle River, NJ: Prentice Hall.

Tulshyan, R. (2010) 'Singapore: The hottest (little) economy in the world', *Time*, 31 July 2010, http://content.time.com/time/business/article/0,8599,2007470,00.html [accessed on 17 January 2017].

Yang, C. (2016) 'Insead pips Harvard to become top MBA school', *Straits Times*, 26 January 2016, www.straitstimes.com/singapore/education/insead-pips-harvard-to-become-top-mba-school [accessed on 17 January 2017].

Yeh, R.S. (1988) 'On Hofstede's treatment of Chinese and Japanese values', *Asia Pacific Journal of Management*, 6(1): 149–160.

Yeh, R. S. and Lawrence, J. (1995) 'Individualism and Confucian dynamism: A note on Hofstede's cultural root to economic growth', *Journal of International Business Studies*, 3: 655–669.

Zhang, Y.M. (1994) 'Leadership attributes in a cultural setting in Singapore', *International Journal of Educational Management*, 8(6): 16–18.

7 Business leaders and leadership in China

Introduction

China had a population of over 1.38 billion at the end of 2016.[1] The scale and pace of its economic growth and societal transformation have been unprecedented since around 1980 (Aoki and Wu, 2012; Warner, 2014). China's GDP in 1978 was only US$216.8 billion, a quarter of that of the United States. Since then economic reforms and opening-up have created three decades of remarkable economic growth at an average rate of 9.8 per cent per year until 2014. Between 1991 and 2011, China's annual GDP growth rate reached more than 9 per cent; however, the 1997/1998 Asian financial crisis adversely affected its GDP growth rates from 1998 to 2001. As shown in Table 7.1, the country's GDP in 2015 reached US$11.01 trillion and GDP per capita US $8,027. The foreign direct investment (FDI) inflow and outflow continued at a moderate upward trend from 1995, with the growth rate accelerating after China joined the World Trade Organization (WTO) in 2011. The inward flow reached US$1,220,903 million and the outward flow US$1,010,202 million in 2015.

Table 7.1 Economic, business and social indicators in China in 2015

GDP (US$ trillion)	11.01	Average disposable income (RMB)	31,195
GDP per capita (US$)	8,027	Corruption index (1–100)	37
Global competitive score (1–7)	4.9	Corruption rank (out of 168)	83
Global competitive rank (out of 144)	28	FDI inward stocks (US$ million)	1,220,903
Global opportunity rank (out of 136)	52	FDI outward stocks (US$ million)	1,010,202

Sources: China Statistics Yearbook 2015; Corruption Perceptions Index 2015; Global Competitiveness Report 2015–2016; Global Opportunity Index 2015; National Bureau of Statistics of the People's Republic of China 2015; World Bank 2015; World Investment Report 2016.

China is now being considered by some analysts and media reporters as the largest economy in the world, surpassing the United States, according to the 2014 purchasing parity power (PPP) GDP figures released by the World Bank and the International Monetary Fund (IMF). China, however, is quick to deny its leading position and re-emphasizes that it is still a 'developing country'. Putting aside the methodology used to estimate its price levels and hence GDP, China has many issues and challenges to cope with domestically (Warner, 2014). For instance, the country's economic growth rate is slowing to the lowest level in almost 25 years. For the first time over the previous 12 years (2000–2011), the annual GDP growth rate in 2012 slowed down below 8 per cent to 7.7 per cent. It continued to slip to 6.9 per cent in 2015 – the first time below 7 per cent since 2009 – and to 6.5 per cent in 2016. Although these rates are reasonably larger than in many of the other countries in the world, China has not been able to meet the official targeted growth rate of 7 per cent set in its 12th Five-Year Plan (2011–2015). The country's top leadership, however, has demonstrated an increasing tolerance for a slower GDP growth rate, and has emphasized the imperative of the 'second transition' from a low-end, labour-intensive and export-led economy to a higher-end, value-added and consumer/service-led economy (BBC, 2015; Bottelier, 2007). Indeed, slowing economic growth is contextualized in the aftermath of the global financial crisis which led to, or occurred in parallel with, a number of domestic challenges, such as a struggling manufacturing industry and volatile stock market.

Nonetheless, China aspires to continue enhancing its economy and improve people's livelihood. The current President, Xi Jinping, officially introduced the concept of the 'China Dream' on 29 November 2012 to set the momentum for national rejuvenation. Its goals are to build a moderately prosperous society in all respects by the centenary of the Communist Party of China (CPC) in 2021, and to develop China into a modern socialist country that is prosperous, strong, democratic, culturally advanced and harmonious by the centenary of the People's Republic of China (PRC) in 2049 (Ross, 2015). China has certainly made noticeable progress towards national rejuvenation. Based on the Global Competitiveness Report 2015–2016, China scored 4.9 on a 1–7 point system, ranking 28th out of 140 economies in the world. This report assesses the level of productivity as determined by the confluence of institutions, infrastructure, macro-economic environments, health and education, goods market efficiency, financial and labour markets, technology and innovation, market size and business sophistication.

China's overall competitiveness, however, suffers from several limitations, a prominent institutional factor being corruption. As shown in Table 7.1, it ranked 83th out of 168 countries and territories in terms of the level of public sector corruption. An inadequate legal institutional framework is another limiting factor. For instance, the legal infrastructure, coupled with the protection of property rights and investor rights, places the country only in the middle range of the 144 countries compared.

Within this context, the country's continued transition and emerging challenges mean that business managers have to deal with previously unheard of concepts and that their leadership knowledge, skills and attributes are in urgent need of improvement. Managerial leadership is important to sustain China's growth because of its potential impact on employee and organizational motivation, as well as behaviour and performance. Positional leadership in the lower management hierarchy can be related to individual employee performance and subjective wellbeing, and those at the middle and senior levels may extend their impact to team and organization levels (see Hiller and Beauchesne, 2014).

Indeed the shortage of qualified managerial leaders is a recurrent theme among companies operating in China, regardless of their ownership, size or location. An ideal managerial leader today is expected to simultaneously cope with multiple, sometimes competing, demands, such as communicating in both Chinese and English, understanding both Chinese and Western-imported cultures and values, and managing both domestic and global markets. McKinsey's research estimates that at the higher end of the labour market, in 2020 there will be a shortage of 24 million high-skilled employees and that the opportunity-cost of not filling this gap could reach about US $250 billion, approximately 2.3 per cent of GDP (Chen et al., 2013). Professor Katherine Xin at the top-ranked China Europe International Business School (CEIBS) further estimated during her interview with the *Financial Times* that 'mainland Chinese executives capable of operating at the highest level of global companies still number in the low thousands only' (Hill, 2013).

The dynamic economic, social and cultural contexts in which business managers operate, coupled with the urgent need to update managerial leadership, provides the justification and the space for our focus on China in this chapter. The central tasks are to: (1) identify the changing patterns of managerial leadership from the historical, cultural, political and economic perspectives; and (2) evaluate the available means to develop managerial leadership both from a top-down and a bottom-up perspective.

In order to address these tasks, this chapter starts with a brief introduction of the country, setting managerial leadership in context. It proceeds to explore what managerial leadership means in China, what managerial leaders do and why they do what they do. We take the view that leadership is a process of social influence (Uhl-Bien, 2006), and therefore any investigation of leadership cannot provide a full picture without connecting with past tradition and the evolving society. A number of challenges against the backdrop of the 'second transition' are highlighted to help readers comprehend and potentially find a solution to address these challenges. We believe there is no 'one-size-fits-all' solution to fulfil the shortfall of competent leadership. To this end, we explore various means which individual managers and/or their organizations can use to effectively develop required leadership competencies in a timely, flexible and cost-effective manner.

Traditional normative values on leadership

Before explicating what constitutes qualified managerial leadership in China, a good point of departure at this stage is to ask what *leadership* means in the country. Despite this being an obvious question, it is not easy to articulate. As our previous publication (e.g. Ren et al., 2015) observes, leadership is translated as *ling dao* in China. The word *ling dao*, however, has multiple meanings: it can be used as a noun to describe a leader or a position; as a verb to entail leading and directing; or as an adjective to delineate leaders' qualities and attributes.

The ambiguous use of the language is an indication of the Chinese way of thinking and doing. The characteristic Chinese mental process has a relatively higher tolerance for ambiguity and elasticity compared to that in typical Western culture, and allows room for bounded rationality (Lin and Ho, 2009). On the one hand, this factor points to the 'relational orientation', deeply rooted in Chinese tradition, in which people engage in the relational orientation and therefore consider a range of interconnected factors in a holistic manner (Warner, 2010; Warner, 2011). On the other hand, the tendency to engage in ambiguous discourse can be seen as a way to negotiate and redefine interpersonal positions without directly challenging *a priori* relationship structures (Chang, 1999). In the realm of leadership, this legacy of the Chinese way of thinking and doing constitutes implicit expectations of what managers should do to effectively perform their leadership role.

Just as globalization promotes the convergence and divergence debate in the institution and management literature, discussions in the leadership literature can also be divided into those focusing on the global presence of common leadership attributes and those emphasizing contextual details. A primary example of the first category is the GLOBE study (House et al., 2004) in which researchers have studied 25 societies in search of commonality of leadership characteristics. Mintzberg and cross-cultural scholars, however, revealed these insights and argued that leadership is a fundamentally different process in different cultures (Jackson and Parry, 2011). Kempster and Parry (2011, p. 109) further commented that:

> If indeed leadership is a contextually based process of social influence, then arguably the only 'truth' that is universal is that all such universal leadership theories are fallible and could be disproved in the sense that all contexts are in some way unique. That is not to say that leadership is not real and does not have an effect. Rather, we emphasize the rather ubiquitous belief that the effect and manifestation of leadership varies by context and is perceived relatively.

Therefore, if we are to explain the manifestation of contextualized managerial leadership in China, we need to take a historical approach to connect its past and present (see Warner 2017; Warner and Zhu, 1998). Managerial leadership, or more precisely leadership in the business sector, is not a product of contemporary China. The Western sense of leadership may seem on the surface to have been introduced only after economic reforms and opening-up in the 1980s, but the concept of the market may well have emerged as early as the 16th century (see Faure, 2006).

Business enterprise development can be categorized into four stages: namely an imperial era; a period of warfare, such as the anti-Japanese invasion and civil war against the KMT; the foundation of New China; and the period after economic reforms and opening-up. Correspondingly, the perceptions and practice of effective leadership shift alongside these changes in the political and economic realms. Specifically in the imperial system, people's mindsets and behavioural norms are heavily influenced by the traditional religious-philosophical systems, the prominent ones being Confucianism, Daoism, Legalism and Buddhism. Our previous publication has provided a detailed and comprehensive review of these schools of thought and their implications for leadership (see Ren et al., 2015). In short, Confucianism emphasizes the unity of society (hence duty and morality), whereas Daoism elaborates the fluid and changing nature of society. Correspondingly, Confucian leaders find themselves secure in the social hierarchy around them, whereas Daoist leaders respect expression, rather than repression, of members in the group (Lin et al., 2013). In Daoism leaders are collectively expected to practise personal virtues of benevolence and righteousness, as role models, and at the same time allow flexibility to cope with environmental uncertainty. Legalism reinforces rules universally (hence punishment and rewards). A Legalist leader uses positional power to achieve his/her influence (Ma and Tsui, 2015). By the late imperial period, Buddhism was well established in Chinese society, and its religious quest to alleviate suffering by purifying the mind and attaining enlightenment encouraged people to practise virtues and have a good heart and right intentions. The syncretic tendencies of these traditional influences point to a holistic orientation, with an emphasis on harmony and the doctrine of means, as well as a social order built upon hierarchy. Hence, a typical Chinese leader, influenced by these traditional values, endorses positive relationships among teams, is humanely oriented and avoids conflicts.

To some extent, modern-day 'managerial leadership' in the business sense was largely suppressed or downplayed in pre-modern China, as commodity-exchange is seen as 'parasitic' in Chinese traditional culture (Moody, 2011). Nonetheless, marketplace transactions are not non-existent and economic modernization occurred before the foundation of New China. In fact, the new cultural movement marked by the May Fourth Movement at the end of the imperial era awakened the call for cultural overhaul in which traditional cultures, especially Confucianism, were seen as the root cause of China's failing status compared to the Western world. The Republican period which followed introduced Western technology (e.g. the construction of railways), paving the way for an encounter with Western managerial culture and systems.

However, it was not until the economic reforms and opening-up (*gaige kaifang*) officially started in 1979 that the world's attention was drawn to China's unprecedented growth. These reforms have restructured the previously centrally planned economy to a market-oriented economy and have encouraged the participation of non-state economic entities. Correspondingly, effective managerial leadership qualities shifted from being ideologically driven to increasingly market oriented. After the foundation of the New China in 1949, the assignment and selection of leaders in the political system was heavily ideologically driven. Being both 'red and expert' (*you hong you zhuan*) key requirements of leaders in the public sector and the state-owned enterprises (SOEs) that constituted the national economy (Warner, 2014). 'Red' meant having the right political orientation, whereas 'expert' meant being equipped with technical skills. The sentiments reflected in this slogan, however, eroded after the introduction of economic reforms towards market orientation. Our previous book (Ren et al., 2015) has detailed the factory managers' responsibility system (*chang zhang fu ze zhi*) and the one leader control system (*yi zhang zhi*). The reforms since 1978 have exposed Chinese businesses and business leaders to previously unheard of concepts such as competition and profitability. Performance-, results- and transaction-driven leadership has since flourished, incorporating more transformational and value-based leadership practices and styles, as will be discussed in the next section.

Influence of Western management practices

The mainstream leadership styles derived from the West exist to varying degrees in China, firstly, due to the increasing trade and cultural exchanges and, secondly, due to the compatibility with China's traditional cultures. For instance, Confucianism's active leadership bears much resemblance to transformational leadership in which a managerial leader motivates employees to assume more responsibilities and pursue higher goal attainment through personalized consideration and intellectual stimulation (see Warner, 2016). Transformational leadership is particularly useful when interacting with the young generation, which is more confident, precocious, independent and self-centred (Jiang, 2013). The need for self-fulfilment makes this generation less tolerant of authoritarian, abusive or exploitative leadership.

Value-based leadership styles, such as servant leadership and authentic leadership, fit Daoism's doctrine of no action and selflessness. Servant leadership empowers employees to pursue their development, whereas authentic leadership accepts the limitations (and strengths) of the self and subordinates, and allows for appropriate action to be taken (Ma and Tsui, 2016). Again, the employee-centric orientation embedded in these leadership styles corresponds with the changing nature of China's workforce. In our study of 594 young-generation employees, we found that they prefer leadership styles that meet their need for involvement. Therefore, there is a strong preference for leaders who provide timely feedback and demonstrate respect and recognition.

Nonetheless, the adoption of Western management practices is contingent upon organizations' specificity. A useful proxy to categorize differences in the perceptions and practices of effective leadership is by way of organizational ownership structure. Western leadership theories find their place mostly in foreign-invested companies in which the corporate structure and human resources management (HRM) systems are influenced by their Western head-quarters. Managerial leaders are recruited based on competency, and mainly comprise those who have returned from overseas or have familiarity with Western cultures and values (Warner, 2014). Senior leaders of large SOEs are increasingly better educated compared to those in the centrally planned system. However, given the ideological and traditional influences, these leaders are expected to combine transactional leadership with paternalism.

China's vibrant private sector is not generated by free-market forces, as Tsui and colleagues observe, since the market is not truly free for private enterprises. Rather, the private sector is a result of the 'visible hands' of Chinese entrepreneurs (Tsui et al., 2017, p. 5) through their hard work, network building and maintenance, and constant adaptation. Many of the initial private entrepreneurs are ex-managers or employees in SOEs (see the review of the *xia hai* phenomenon, i.e. jumping into the sea, in Ren et al., 2015). While these entrepreneurs are drawn to Western-derived market competition, they draw heavily on management practices and leadership styles in state-owned enterprises for inspiration. Owners or managers as agents of the owners, lead by means of a hands-on and holistic approach. Relationship-building with external stakeholders, including the government, is particularly important for small and medium-sized private enterprises (SMEs).

In addition, top business leaders and managers in companies at all levels and with different ownership structures have also been under growing pressure to deal with unprecedented challenges in a global context, making global mindsets and cross-cultural capabilities pivotal to their survival and success. This requirement is particularly critical considering China's second transition up the value chain. Increasingly, business managers need to simultaneously consider short- and long-term goals within the global context, and accord greater emphasis on innovative behaviours from their employees.

Another key aspect of Western leadership theory that is worth noting is ethical leadership. To some extent corporate governance has made positive advancement in Chinese companies. Leading by practising and promoting normatively appropriate behaviours (i.e. ethical leadership) resembles on the surface China's traditional emphasis on morality. However, the definition of ethical leadership differs in China from that in typical Western countries (Resick et al., 2011). Compared to the Western emphasis on following clearly defined rules, Chinese implicit theories of leadership are more elastic and relational. Leaders are more likely to adapt their behaviour and performance benchmark pragmatically. For instance, Jiang and Zhu (2013) found in their study on food security in China that, although companies have the intention of producing high-quality and safe food products, they are prepared to make compromises. The pressure to minimize costs, driven by price competition and a lack of state regulation enforcement, impedes managers' commitment to social responsibility. In a cross-cultural study on ethical leadership, Resick and colleagues found that Chinese managers listed consideration and respect for others as the most important characteristics of ethical leaders, followed by personal character and fairness. In contrast, their American counterparts rated personal character as the most important characteristic of ethical leaders, followed by accountability, consideration and respect for others.

Tension

As can be seen, the key challenges for managerial leadership are closely related to economic, social and societal changes taking place in China amidst the effects of globalization. During our fieldwork in China, we noticed that managers at different levels of the management hierarchy often feel overwhelmed by the scope and range of market changes and business demands. They are thus keen to seek inspirational business leaders who have demonstrated effective leadership qualities that have led them to success, wealth and fame.

Jack Ma, founder and executive chairman of Alibaba, the world's leading e-commerce company, is among the most popular 'role-models' frequently referred to by our interviewees. Jack Ma was a school teacher before he founded Alibaba. Now the company goes beyond providing an online shopping platform; it has significantly influenced Chinese consumers' way of shopping, banking and taking out insurance. To make this happen, Jack Ma has demonstrated qualities that are normally associated with effectively leadership, including, for instance, vision, transform, passion, innovation, persistence and risk-taking. In addition to these qualities, our interviewees pointed out his global mindset which has allowed him to integrate Western technology into the Chinese local market. Jack Ma became familiar with the internet for the first time during his trip to the United States in 1995, and has since introduced internet business to Chinese consumers.

A global mindset is seen by our interviewees as particularly significant for dealing with today's challenges. As previously noted, China is endeavouring to upgrade its economy throughout the value chain – and this is clearly happening. A report by the Asian Development Bank dated December 2015 shows that approximately one-third of the country's exports are now high-tech products, used, for instance, in the railway, nuclear power, shipbuilding and telecommunications sectors. By 2014 China had overtaken Japan to become the largest exporter of high-tech products in Asia, with a 43.7 per cent share (Gao et al., 2016). Given that exports of high-tech products are now a key driver of the Chinese economy, a further issue for its companies is whether they are equipped with managers who are capable of engaging with overseas operations at the higher end of the value chain.

China's ongoing encounter with Western management practices has created a greater demand for professional managers. The question, however, is to what extent women take up these leadership roles. A slogan popularized by the former Chinese leader, Chairman Mao – that 'women hold up half the sky' in the new socialist society – has long been in existence, but still remains an idealist illusion (Xie and Zhu, 2016). Nevertheless, there has been encouraging advancement. The proportion of female CEOs in publicly listed firms on the Shanghai and Shenzhen Stock Exchanges increased from 4.6 per cent in 1997 to 5.6 per cent in 2010 (Zhang, 2012). In 2013, women held 51 per cent of senior management positions in China, significantly higher than the global trend of 24 per cent (Lagerberg, 2013). A number of contributing factors can be identified, including increasing educational attainment by women, decreasing fertility rates and sectoral changes that gave rise to opportunities for women in the labour force (Rowley and Yukongdi, 2008). The positive improvement is certainly welcomed by women, as illustrated in a large-scale study of 296 individual women managers recently conducted by Xie and Zhu (2016). The authors found that the participants were generally satisfied with the proportion of women in managerial roles, and that they were content with their own promotion possibilities within the current organization.

Despite the relatively higher proportion of female managers, the 'glass ceiling' effect still prevails, often at the unconscious level, constituting obstacles and challenges that confront females, but not their male counterparts, in the progression to leadership roles. Women managers are often associated with industries that are stereotypically viewed as female-dominant. In publicly listed firms, gender change from male to female in CEO succession is found to disrupt the succession process, and adversely influences post-succession firm performance (Zhang and Qu, 2016). In fact, most women CEOs in China are either the founders of the company or have inherited it from their fathers (Zhang, 2012). Women's participation in leadership roles in state-owned enterprises is lower than in non-state owned enterprises. In addition, there is consistent evidence of gender-based pay gaps when females and males have the same pay-determining characteristics (Xiu and Gunderson, 2014).

Research on female leadership in China initially emerged in the 1980s, with a focus on female cadres in the public sector, and later developed quickly to encompass female managers in the business sector. Gender equality is one of the key policies of the Communist Party, which aims at liberating women and encouraging their participation in different sectors of society (Cho et al., 2015). In the business sector, flexible working arrangements, the presence of other female leaders in senior leadership teams and a supportive organizational culture are reported to help mitigate the stereotypical biases against women (e.g. Xie and Zhu, 2015; Zhang and Qu, 2016).

Leader development

Developing managerial leadership can take many forms. The conventional knowledge of leadership development is fundamentally a top-down approach in the sense that training programmes are initiated and organized by companies. During our interviews, we found that very often training plans in companies are formulated by the HR department, and the provision of training is used as a motivational tool for the promising 'star' employees. Research adopting the top-down approach has yielded a plethora of studies in both leadership development literature and human resource development literature (see, for instance, Day and Dragoni, 2015, for a recent review). Common interests of these studies include attempts to understand motivation to participate in training, evaluation of training programmes and transfer of training.

Institutes providing MBA, EMBA and executive training have flourished in recent years, thus gaining foreign experiences (see Warner and Goodall 2009). At the start of the 21st century, there were only around 60 institutes offering MBA and EMBA programmes (Zhao et al., 2004). Within less than two decades, China's MBA programmes, offered on the mainland and in Hong Kong SAR, have grown to become internationally renowned, with seven institutes included in the *Financial Times* Top 100 Global MBA Ranking in 2016: namely the HKUST Business School, CEIBS, CUHK Business School, Shanghai Jiao Tong University: Antai, Renmin University of China School of Business, University of Hong Kong and Fudan University School of Management. With regard to EMBA offerings, this qualification has proven to be a clear preference for international partnerships, particularly with institutes in the US, despite being a young market. There are 15 programmes offered either by Chinese institutions alone or through international partnerships and included in the *FT* Top 100 Global EMBA Ranking in 2016, namely: Kellogg/HKUST Business School; Tsinghua University/INSEAD; Washington-Fudan; Shanghai Jiao Tong University Antai; Ceibs Global; University of Chicago Booth; Kedge-SJTU Global; OneMBA: Xiamen/RSM/UNC/FGV São Paulo/Egade; Arizona State University Carey-SNAI; CUHK Business School; BI Norwegian Business School/Fudan University School of Management; Fudan University School of Management; University of Hong Kong (HKU-Fudan International); Western University Ivey; and Tongji University/ENPC.

The above-mentioned strong momentum is partly due to the growing need for advanced managerial know-how and developing a global mindset on the market-demand side, and is partly facilitated by increasingly qualified faculty members and international collaborations on the market-supply side. Nonetheless, there is growing criticism of the quality of these programmes, with students questioning the lack of localization and isomorphism of programmes offered by different institutes. Although the Western-based teaching materials open up scientific management to Chinese managers, their everyday work is built upon the Chinese way of thinking, doing and interacting. Some managers resort to classic Chinese approaches for answers. Since 2007 there has indeed been a wave of interest in learning classic Chinese philosophies (*guoxue*), which were soon incorporated into the MBA, EMBA and executive training programmes. The focus is on a historic account of events and systems in Chinese civilization which provide experience and guidance on how to solve practical issues today. Researchers have also shown a greater interest in trying to understand the role of traditional Chinese philosophies in HRM, business operations and the internationalization of Chinese firms (e.g. Busse et al., 2016; Zhang et al., 2016).

Additionally, the EMBA market is particularly affected by China's recent anti-corruption campaign in which managerial leaders in the public sector and state-owned enterprises have been prohibited from enrolling in training programmes with high tuition fees (Xinhuanet, 2014). Intense pressure is thus placed on the EMBA providers to attract prospective students and work on innovating the content and delivery of programmes.

Another training avenue with 'Chinese characteristics' is the Party School, which focuses not only on *ganbu* (cadres) in government, but also on managerial leaders in enterprises. In our interview with a municipal-level Party School in a medium-sized city in China, we were advised that the annual training plan involved, for instance:

- cadres at the county level (*xian ji gan bu*);
- leaders at section level or equivalent (*ke ji ling dao gan bu*);
- young and middle-aged cadres (*zhong qing nian gan bu*);
- female cadres (*nv ganbu*);
- high-quality talent with creative capabilities (*gao ceng ci chuang xin xing ren cai*); and
- managerial leaders of enterprises (*qi ye ling dao ren yuan*).

These enterprises are mainly state owned, with some directly managed by the municipal governments.

Despite different audiences, the approach to and content of training, as we were informed, did not vary considerably. The primary goal of the training was to study 'socialist theory with Chinese characteristics' and the core value systems of socialism. These training sessions lasted about one week and took the form of residential learning. Apart from the focus on understanding the principles specified at the most recently concluded CPC National Congress, the training session provided to company leaders included finance and taxation policies, financial management, human resources management, construction of organizational culture and protection of intellectual property.

The effectiveness of these sessions is questionable; take the timetable of the nine-day training programme for instance: there appears to be a huge gap between what is urgently required of managerial leaders, as mentioned above, and what is offered in the Party School. Only 5 per cent of the time was allocated to contents pertinent to the economic system and industrial upgrading; 22 per cent of the time was allocated to facilitating self-reflection and network-building amongst participants. The vast majority of the time (73 per cent) was allocated to ideological orientation, including, for instance, studying classic socialist works, the historical experience of the CPC and current government directives. Pedagogically, the training primarily took the form of lectures (68 per cent) complemented occasionally by group discussions (16 per cent) and video illustrations (11 per cent) and, to a further lesser extent, by self-study (5 per cent).

Another key avenue for leader development is initiated by individuals in a bottom-up approach. Based on our years of experience in the research field, we would argue that developing managerial leadership is not a responsibility of companies alone. Our observations (e.g. Ren et al., 2014; Ren et al., 2015) concur with a recent review of the learning literature where Noe et al. (2015) comment that individuals are active agents acquiring knowledge and skills deemed appropriate for career progression. Indeed, within the context of China, firms appear uncommitted to developing their managers' abilities (Lamond and Zheng, 2010; Shen, 2010); and even when companies do provide training, they are unable to address the multiplicity of requirements for the development of quality leadership in a timely and cost-effective manner (Warner and Goodall, 2009). Therefore, scholars and practitioners have called for self-development as a viable solution to competence development and organizational learning in general (Fang, 2010).

Understandings of a self-initiated form of leadership development in China, however, are very limited, with research on this issue still at a nascent stage. Our previous publications (e.g. Ren et al., 2014; Ren et al., 2015) are the first of their kind to provide a systematic investigation of contextual enablers and individual predictors for this developmental strategy. For readers who are interested, we also provided a detailed examination of specific leadership skills that managerial leaders focus on in their self-developmental activities. We will not repeat these here; instead, we will bundle a number of individual characteristics validated in Western literature and analyse them in the Chinese context. By doing so, we hope to provide practical benefits for organizations when they design recruitment and selection personality tests.

People displaying a social-oriented bundle of characteristics tend to pay attention to external changing environments, which they keep updated through constantly revaluating their leadership competencies. The social-oriented bundle of individual characteristics refers to people's tendency to acquire and value knowledge from their social environment. Such a tendency is rooted, for instance, in one's seeking feedback from others, being open to new experiences, being ready for change and possessing social complexity. Compared to those working in relatively conservative regions such as Xi'an, participants in more open regions such as Beijing and Shanghai tend to fall into this category. As relatively more channels are available to obtain feedback, these managers are better positioned to perceive developmental needs and their subsequent personal responsibility to develop a full range of leadership competencies.

We also identified people failing within the learning-oriented bundle, which refers to a set of individual characteristics that reflect one's inclination to learn, and these people's valence to learning itself. Such inclination is rooted, for instance, in the extent of one's curiosity and tolerance for ambiguity. As the literature suggests, people displaying this bundle of characteristics engage in self-discovery, respond adaptively and persist in the face of obstacles and challenges (Kang et al., 2009). These groups of people may not be as fully aware or connected with their changing society as social-oriented participants. They have learned to achieve self-perfection and self-fulfilment, and have used themselves as a 'comparison group'.

In contrast, self-oriented participants seem not to pay attention to changes in their surroundings, including their dealings with others. Therefore, they either do not seek to obtain social competencies, or feel they have sufficient knowledge of these competencies. The self-oriented bundle refers to a set of individual characteristics pertinent to the extent to which people are self-aware with respect to their abilities of cognition, emotion and control of personal cognitive processes. These people show little interest in recognizing personal responsibility in the learning process.

Similar reactions were recorded in relation to the ambiguous linkage between the career-oriented bundle of individual characteristics and the ethical domain of leadership competencies. The career-oriented bundle is defined here as a set of individual characteristics reflecting the centrality of, and preference for, work in one's life. It can have three foci: the career (e.g. career orientation and career exploration), the job (e.g. job engagement) and the organization (e.g. organizational commitment). All participants studied confirmed that the ethical domain was not well nurtured or supported in their organization. For instance, ethics were not incorporated into performance appraisal systems; nor were they clearly communicated within the organization or rewarded in compensation packages and promotion plans. All of these factors influenced self-regulatory mechanisms comprising self-evaluation and responsibility appraisal. Therefore, in cases in which managers were highly 'career oriented', these managers tended to select and value the factors most relevant and important to their work and careers.

Evaluation and conclusion

The magnitude of complexities inherent in China's current context poses a significant challenge for managerial leaders to effectively perform their leadership roles and flexibly develop capabilities; neither is an easy undertaking, as illustrated above. Paradox emerges as both a theme of the transformational context and a skill required for managers to navigate such a context. In this sense, practising paradoxical leader behaviours becomes useful to cope with the increasing interplay between Chinese and Western business, trade and cultural changes. An effective business leader needs to: combine his/her self-centredness with other-centredness; maintain distance and closeness with various stakeholders; and treat employees uniformly while recognizing employees' need for autonomy, enforcing work requirements while allowing flexibility and maintaining control of decisions, at the same time allowing participation (Zhang et al., 2016).

A natural question follows as to how to nurture paradoxical leader beha-viour. One possible solution is to incorporate holistic thinking in one's cog-nitive scheme to think and act paradoxically. Another possible solution is to make interactions with complexities 'simple, intuitive and pleasurable' through the application of 'design thinking' (Kolko, 2015). Design thinking, refers to a set of principles that involve, for instance, empathy with users, a discipline of prototyping and tolerance for failure. Design thinking has recently been advocated in the Western literature (e.g. Brown, 2008), but has not yet made much headway in the discourse of individual managers, companies and training providers in China. However, we believe this approach provides opportunities to examine complex issues and explore potential solutions in the context of China in a simplifying and humanizing manner.

Another promising area is to nurture 'communities of practice' (CoP). Social learning has recently been advocated in the academic literature (e.g. Noe et al., 2014; Howorth et al., 2015) and its elements are evident, though scattered, in our fieldwork with managers. Throughout our research in China, we noticed over the years the increasing application of social media in a wide range of peo-ple's everyday work and life. The most vibrant example is the rapid development of Wechat, a free messaging application similar to WhatsApp used in Western countries. Many managers in our study have commented on creating Wechat groups and sharing moments in Wechat as a flexible, timely and cost-effective way of connecting with people sharing similar interests, having quick access to knowledge and information, and learning from others. This emerging learning pattern, largely self-initiated, corresponds to the CoP concept (Lave and Wenger, 1991; Wenger, 1998). CoP is a concept within the social theories of learning which views learning as situated in the lived-in world. It would be advisable for companies, industry associations or government to promote the establishment and maintenance of CoP comprising their representatives. Not only does it provide a diversified source for social learning, but it is also consistent with the long-standing Chinese saying: a fence needs the support of three stakes and a capable fellow needs the help of three other people.

Last but not least, China's vibrant business environment has nurtured a growing number of entrepreneurs and professional managers to pursue career development. Women are finding more opportunities to move up the ladder, as evidenced by their relatively higher participation ratio in leadership teams compared to other Asian countries. While this positive advancement is facili-tated by women's greater educational attainment, more fragmented family structures and economic development, the influence of the renascence of tra-ditional culture on their role identity is yet to be known. Furthermore, the varying degrees of adoption of Western management and leadership practices in companies of different ownership types highlight the context-dependent and relational-oriented nature of Chinese implicit schemes. Understanding individual managers' struggles and responses to the country's ongoing transformation therefore requires meaningful contextualization, rather than treating context as a mere background.

Note

1 This figure, estimated by the UN, covers 31 provinces, autonomous regions and direct-controlled municipalities, excluding Hong Kong SAR, Macao SAR and Taiwan. http://data.un.org/CountryProfile.aspx?crName=china.

References

Aoki, M. and Wu, J.L. (2012) *The Chinese Economy: A New Transition*, Basingstoke and New York: Palgrave Macmillan.

BBC (2015) 'China's economic growth slows to 6.9%', 19 October 2015www.bbc.com/news/business-34536052 [accessed on 3 December 2016].

Bottelier, P. (2007) 'China's Economy in 2020: The Challenge of a Second Transition', *Asia Policy*, 4(1): 31–40.

Brown, T. (2008) 'Design thinking', *Harvard Business Review*, https://hbr.org/2008/06/design-thinking [accessed on 4 December 2016].

Busse, R., Warner, M. and Zhao, S. (2016) 'In search of the roots of HRM in the Chinese workplace', *Chinese Management Studies*, 10(3): 527–543.

Chen, L.K., Mourshed, M. and Grant, A. (2013) 'The $250 billion question: Can China close the skills gap?' McKinsey & Co. Report. www.mckinsey.com/industries/social-sector/our-insights/the-250-billion-question-can-china-close-the-skills-gap [accessed on 4 December 2016].

Chang, H. C. (1999) 'The "well-defined" is "ambiguous": Indeterminacy in Chinese conversation', *Journal of Pragmatics*, 31(4): 535–556.

Cho, Y., McLean, G.N., Amornpipat, I., Chang, W., Hewapathirana, G.I., Horimoto, M., Lee, M.M., Li, J., Manikoth, N.N., Othman, J. and Hamzah, S.R. (2015) 'Asian women in top management: Eight country cases', *Human Resource Development International*, 18(4): 407–428.

Faure, D. (2006) *China and Capitalism: A History of Business Enterprise in Modern China*, Hong Kong: Hong Kong University Press.

Day, D. and Dragoni, L. (2015) 'Leadership development: An outcome-oriented review based on time and levels of analyses', *Annual Review of Organizational Psychology and Organizational Behavior*, 2: 133–156.

Fang, Y.F. (2010) *Lang Xing Zhong Ceng: Zhong Ceng Yue De Li, Lao Ban Yue Qing Song* (Wolfy Middle Managers: The More Competent Middle Managers Are, the More Relaxed Bosses Are), Guangzhou: Guangdong Provincial Publishing Group.

Gao, Y., Zhong, N. and Lyu, C. (2016) 'China moves up the exports value chain', *China Daily*, 7 January 2016. http://wap.chinadaily.com.cn/2016-01/07/content_22966367.htm [accessed on 19 December 2016].

Hill, A. (2013) 'The only fix for China's managerial shortage', *Financial Times*, 29 April 2013. www.ft.com/intl/cms/s/0/efb237ec-adb6-11e2-82b8-00144feabdc0.html#axzz3uo02aUAk [accessed on 20 December 2016].

House, R.J., Hanges, P.J., Javidan, M., Dorfman, P.W. and Gupta, V. (2004) *Culture, Leadership and Organizations: The GLOBE Study of 62 Societies*, Thousand Oaks, CA: Sage.

Howorth, C., Smith, S.M. and Parkinson, C. (2015) 'Social learning and social entrepreneurship education', *Academy of Management Learning & Education*, 11(3): 371–389.

Jackson, B. and Parry, K. (2011) *A Very Short, Fairly Interesting and Reasonably Cheap Book about Studying Leadership* (2nd edn), London: Sage.

Jiang, Q.J. and Zhu, Y. (2013) 'Confronting the crisis of food safety and revitalizing companies' social responsibility in China', *Asia Pacific Business Review*, 19(4): 600–616.

Jiang, X. (2013) 'The new generation of migrant workers in labour market in China', in E. Pries (ed.), *Shifting Boundaries of Belonging and New Migration Dynamics in Europe and China*, Basingstoke: Palgrave Macmillan, pp. 164–185.

Kang, M.J., Hsu, M., Krajbich, I.M., Loewenstein, G., McClure, S.M. and Wang, J.T., (2009) 'The wick in the candle of learning: Epistemic curiosity activates reward circuitry and enhances memory', *Psychological Science*, 20(8): 963–973.

Kempster, S. and Parry, K. (2011) 'Grounded theory and leadership research: A critical realist perspective', *Leadership Quarterly*, 22(1): 106–120.

Kolko, J. (2015) 'Design thinking comes of age', *Harvard Business Review*, September 2015, https://hbr.org/2015/09/design-thinking-comes-of-age [accessed on 12 December 2016].

Lamond, D. and Zheng, C. (2010) 'HRM research in China: Looking back and looking forward', *Chinese Human Resource Management*, 1: 6–16.

Lagerberg, F. (2013) *International Business Report: Women in Senior Management*. www.grantthornton.global/en/insights/articles/women-in-business-2013/ [accessed on 19 April 2017].

Lave, J. and Wenger, E. (1991) *Situated Learning: Legitimate Peripheral Participation*, Cambridge: Cambridge University Press.

Lin, L.H. and Ho, Y.L. (2009) 'Confucian dynamism, cultural and ethical changes in Chinese societies: A comparative study of China, Taiwan and Hong Kong', *International Journal of Human Resource Management*, 20(11): 2402–2417.

Lin, L.H., Ho, Y.L. and Lin, W.H.E. (2013) 'Confucian and Taoist work values: An exploratory study of the Chinese transformational leadership behavior', *Journal of Business Ethics*, 113: 91–103.

Ma, L., and Tsui, A. (2015) 'Traditional Chinese philosophies and contemporary leadership', *Leadership Quarterly*, 26: 13–24.

Moody, P. R. (2011) 'Han Fei in his context: Legalism on the eve of the Qin conquest', *Journal of Chinese Philosophy*, 38(1): 14–30.

Hiller, N.J. and Beauchesne, M. M. (2014) 'Executive leadership: CEOs, top management teams, and organizational-level outcomes', in D. Day (ed.), *The Oxford Handbook of Leadership and Organizations*, New York: Oxford University Press, pp. 556–588.

Noe, R.A., Clarke, A.D.M. and Klein, H.J. (2014) 'Learning in the twenty-first-century workplace', *Annual Review of Organizational Psychology and Organizational Behavior*, 1: 245–275.

Ren, S., Wood, R. and Zhu, Y. (2014) 'Winning the talent war in China with DIY learning', *MIT Sloan Management Review*, 56(1): 19–21.

Ren, S., Wood, R. and Zhu, Y. (2015) *Business Leadership Development in China*, London and New York: Routledge.

Resick, C., Gillian, M., Mary, K., Marcus, D., Ho, K. and Chunyan, P. (2011) 'What ethical leadership means to me: Asian, American, and European perspectives', *Journal of Business Ethics*, 101(3): 435–457

Ross, J. (2015) 'China's Five Year Plan to achieve a 'moderately prosperous society', *China.org.cn*, 30 October. www.china.org.cn/opinion/2015-10/30/content_36935303.htm [accessed on 20 December 2016].

Rowley, C. and Yukongdi, V. (eds) (2008) *The Changing Face of Women Managers in Asia*, London and New York: Routledge.

Shen, J. (2010) 'Employees' satisfaction with HRM in Chinese privately-owned enterprises', *Asia Pacific Business Review*, 16(3): 339–354.

Tsui, A.S., Zhang, Y. and Chen, X.P. (2017) *Leadership of Chinese Private Enterprises: Insights and Interviews*, London: Palgrave Macmillan.

Uhl-Bien, M. (2006) 'Relational leadership theory: Exploring the social processes of leadership and organizing', *Leadership Quarterly*, 17(6): 654–676.

Warner, M. (2010) 'In search of Confucian HRM: Theory and practice in Greater China and beyond', *International Journal of Human Resource Management*, 21: 2053–2078.

Warner, M. (2014) *Understanding Management in China: Past, Present and Future*, London and New York: Routledge.

Warner, M. (2016) 'Whither "Confucian management"?', *Frontiers of Philosophy in China*, 11(4): 608–632.

Warner, M. (ed.) (2011) *Confucian HRM in Greater China: Theory and Practice*, London and New York: Routledge.

Warner, M. (ed.) (2017) *The Diffusion of Western Economic Ideas in East Asia*, London and New York: Routledge.

Warner, M. and Goodall, K. (eds) (2009) *Management Training and Development in China*, Abingdon and New York: Routledge.

Warner, M. and Zhu, Y. (1998) 'Re-assessing Chinese management: The influence of indigenous versus exogenous models', *Human Systems Management*, 17(4): 245–255.

Wenger, E. (1998) *Communities of Practice: Learning, Meaning and Identity*, Cambridge: Cambridge University Press.

Xie, Y.H. and Zhu, Y. (2016) 'Holding up half of the sky: Women managers' view on promotion opportunities at enterprise level in China', *Journal of Chinese Human Resource Management*, 7(1): 45–60.

Xiu, L. and Gunderson, M. (2014) 'Glass ceiling or sticky floor? Quantile regression decomposition of the gender pay gap in China', *International Journal of Manpower*, 35(3): 306–326.

Xinhuanet (2014) *Zhongyang jinzhi ganbu canjia gaoshoufei peixun, EMBA yuanxiao xian tuixuechao* (The Party bans cadres' enrolment in high-intuition training, a wave of withdrawal from EMBA), 15 September 2014. http://news.xinhuanet.com/poli tics/2014-09/15/c_1112474334.htm [accessed on 15 November 2016].

Zhang, M., Gao, Q., Wheeler, J.V. and Kwon, J. (2016) 'Institutional effect on born global firms in China: The role of Sun Tzu's The Art of War strategies', *Journal of Asia Business Studies*, 10(1): 1–19.

Zhang, Y. (2012) 'Lessons for Executive Women from Chinese Boardrooms', *Forbes*, www.forbes.com/sites/forbeswomanfiles/2012/10/09/lessons-for-executive-women-from-chinese-boardrooms/ [accessed on 20 April 2017].

Zhang, Y. and Qu, H. (2016) 'The impact of CEO succession with gender change on firm performance and succession early departure: Evidence from China's publicly listed companies in 1997–2010', *Academy of Management Journal*, 59(5): 1845–1868.

Zhao, C.J., Lei, Y. and Yang, B.Y. (2004) *China Management Education Report*, Beijing: Tsinghua University Press.

8   Business leaders and leadership in Vietnam

Introduction

Vietnam, officially the Socialist Republic of Vietnam, is the easternmost country on the Indochina Peninsula in Southeast Asia. Vietnam is bordered by China to the north, Laos to the northwest, Cambodia to the southwest and Malaysia across the South China Sea to the southeast. It covers a total area of approximately 331,210 km². With an estimated 90.5 million inhabitants in 2014, it is the world's fourteenth most populous country, and the eighth most populous Asian country.

The history of Vietnam was heavily dominated by Imperial China for over a millennium, from 111 BC to AD 939, when an independent Vietnamese state was formed. Successive Vietnamese royal dynasties flourished as the nation expanded geographically and politically into Southeast Asia, until the Indochina Peninsula was colonized by the French in the mid-19th century. Following Japanese occupation in the 1940s, the Vietnamese fought French rule in the First Indochina War, eventually expelling the French in 1954. Thereafter, Vietnam was divided politically into two rival states, North and South Vietnam. Conflict between the two sides intensified in what is known as the Vietnam War. The war ended with a North Vietnamese victory in 1975. Vietnam was then unified under a communist government but remained impoverished and politically isolated. Vietnam's reform transition *(Đổi mới)* was officially launched in December 1986 when regulations and policies aimed at the 'socialist oriented market economy' took effect at the Sixth National Communist Party Congress (Nguyen et al., 2011; Nguyen et al., 2015), although some see the changes as having been introduced earlier (Collins, 2009; Edwards and Phan, 2013; Fforde, 2007). These reforms sought the restructuring of state-owned enterprise (SOE) operations, the liberalization of the economic system and the breaking down of the state sector monopoly (Collins et al., 2012; Warner et al., 2005).

Vietnam has indeed been remarkably successful since it inaugurated many of these reforms; its economy has grown for some decades at an impressive rate of over 7 per cent per annum, the second fastest growth in the region after China (Collins 2011; Warner, 2013). Since 2000, Vietnam's economic growth rate has been among the highest in the world. In 2011, it had the highest Global Growth Generators Index of 11 major economies. In 2015, Vietnam's nominal GDP reached US$191.5 billion, with a nominal GDP per capita of US$2,088 (Table 8.1). Its successful economic reforms resulted in it joining the World Trade Organization (WTO) in 2007. It is also a historical member of the Organisation Internationale de la Francophonie. Vietnam remains one of the world's four remaining one-party socialist states, officially espousing 'communism'.

The economic transition has not only seen an improvement in the effectiveness and productivity of SOEs, but has also created a more 'business-friendly' environment to attract foreign-owned enterprises (FOEs) and nurture domestic private enterprises (DPEs) (Collins et al., 2013). Other areas have seen little visible progress, although Vietnam embarked on deeper economic reforms and the 'three pillar' programme (*Chương trình ba trụ cột kinh tế*) in early 2012, which moved towards the restructuring of public investment, transforming SOEs and modernizing the banking sector. Nevertheless, its economic growth in 2015 reached 6 per cent (see Economist Intelligence Unit, 2015; Leung, 2015).

Vietnam's transition has thus been significantly characterized by a gradualist and incremental approach *en route* to market orientation that aims to stand back from the old state-planned economy (Edwards and Phan, 2013; Warner, 2013; Zhu et al., 2008).

Table 8.1 Economic, business and social indicators in Vietnam (2015–2016)

GDP in 2015 (US$ billion)	191.5	Disposable personal income in 2016 (VND billion)	168
GDP per capita in 2015 (US$)	2088.3	Employed workforce in 2016	53,240,000
Global competitive score in 2015 (1–7)	4.3	Corruption index in 2015 (1–100)	31
Global competitive rank in 2015 (out of 140)	68	Corruption rank in 2015 (out of 175)	112
Global opportunity score in 2015 (1–10)	4.79	FDI inward stocks by the end of 2015 (US$ billion)	102.79
Global opportunity rank in 2015 (out of 136)	86	FDI outward stocks by the end of 2015	N/A

Source: Vietnam: Foreign Investment: https://en.portal.santandertrade.com/establish-overseas/vietnam/investing.

It has furthermore achieved remarkable growth against a backdrop of political stability and continued industrial transformation. More than ever leadership (*khả năng lãnh đạo*) remains an important issue in Vietnam's businesses. The process of economic reform and societal transformation has, in turn, had complex influences on the knowledge, skills and attributes required for management leaders. The complexities are well illustrated in a hybrid economic structure where public and private ownership coexist, each of which has different developmental characteristics and Human Resource Management (HRM) approaches (Zhu et al., 2008). Transforming the competencies of management into relevant and appropriate leadership behaviours thus continues to be a challenge (Edwards and Phan, 2013).

This chapter aims to present the key aspects of business leadership in Vietnam through a qualitative investigation, including secondary data, in-depth interviews with relevant business leaders in two main commercial business centres of Vietnam – Ho Chi Minh and Hanoi – together with related observations. This study is based on data drawn from the 40 interviewees of the 12 case study companies based on three key forms of ownership, including SOEs, DPEs and FOEs. The chapter presents the detailed findings of key themes, including historical and cultural traditions and their impact on business leaders; foreign influence on developing modern practices of business leadership; and the tension between socialist practices and the new concept that has brought about by the FOEs sector since the *Đổi mới* started, as well as challenges to change. Finally, the chapter concludes by evaluating the key aspects and highlighting a number of implications for literature, managerial practice and the direction of future research.

In examining these themes, this chapter is organized as follows. The next section analyses Vietnamese traditional leadership values in order to provide an overview of the impact of cultural context on Vietnamese modern business leadership practices. This account also outlines a brief history of the impact of reforms taking place in Vietnam, focusing particularly on the distinctive historical background of the country. This, in turn, provides a foundation for a subsequent analysis based on the economic, social and cultural contexts relating to the shifting requirements for business leaders. The third section explains the adoption of foreign practices in Vietnamese business units, including reviewing challenges of modern management and leadership. The fourth section explores the tensions between conventional Vietnamese leadership styles and practices, and the adoption and modification of Western leadership concepts at organizational level, in particular the influence of FOEs. The final section offers evaluation and conclusion, focusing on a 'context-specific' explanation based on a holistic approach.

Traditional normative values of leadership

Vietnam's culture and tradition have developed over the centuries from their origins in the indigenous ancient *Đông Sơn* culture. Some elements of the national culture have Chinese origins, drawing on elements of Confucianism and Daoism in its traditional political system and philosophy. The influences of immigrant peoples from the Chine – such as the Cantonese, Hakka, Hokkien and Hainan cultures – can also be seen, while the national religion of Buddhism is strongly entwined with popular culture. Vietnam's history is marked by many invasions, alongside a sense of pride in protecting the country, which has resulted in a belief in the people's own national as well as local cultures. The traditional focuses of Vietnamese culture are humanity (*nhân nghĩa*) and harmony (*hài hòa*); family and community values are highly regarded. The influences of Western cultures, most notably of France and the United States during their respective occupation of the country, are evident in Vietnam. Since the 20th century, the cultural life of Vietnam has been deeply influenced by its socialist government through media and cultural programmes.

One distinctive characteristic of Vietnamese society is that women are given more respect here than in other countries. Vietnam was once a matriarchy, and there are a large number of great heroines. Two of the most popular are the Trung sisters, who led the first national uprising against the Chinese who had conquered Vietnam in the year 40 AD (Reese, 2016). Women played a major role during the country's wars with outsiders, especially during the war against the United States (BBC, 2016). They served as combat soldiers and performed much of the work in the communes, factories and at home while the men were away fighting. Some Vietnamese women have held high positions of authority. In 1973, Madam Nguyen Thi Binh, a communist leader, negotiated at the Paris Peace Conference on behalf of the Democratic Republic of Vietnam, the Northern Vietnam government. During and after the war the government offered to improve women's rights, equitable treatment and representation in government, including the creation of job quotas in 1960 which required that women occupy a certain percentage of jobs in different sectors. Women's role in leadership has continued to increase in contemporary Vietnam, and they have increasing held leadership positions. Between 1992 and 2007, the percentage of women in the National Assembly grew from 18.5 to 27.3 per cent, although in the most recent election women lost ground, holding only 25.7 per cent of the seats in parliament in 2008 (Truong, 2008). Currently, Madam Đặng Thị Ngọc Thịnh is the Vice President of Vietnam, a position she has held since April 2016. Additionally, Madam Nguyễn Thị Kim Ngân was elected as Chairwoman of the National Assembly in March 2016, the first time a woman has ever held the position (Hong, 2016; Chi and Trang, 2016).

Although the Vietnamese adopted the Confucian principle of male superiority, women were regarded as resilient and strong-willed. Women in Vietnam have historically been economically empowered; they have a long tradition of participating actively in the labour force. This is reflected in the high level of women's work participation rate, which is identical to that of men. In villages, women have assumed a great deal of responsibility for the cultivation of paddy fields, often working harder than men and sometimes engaged in retail trade of all kinds. Since *Doi moi*, many working women have performed low-paying factory work. Women account for 80 per cent of the workforce in the textile and garment industry, which has become one of Vietnam's primary export areas. A few women have owned agricultural estates, factories and other businesses, and both urban and rural women have typically managed the family income. Women serve in high-level positions in business and receive the same pay as men in government. Women's leadership in business is growing, and 30 per cent of Board of Director roles in Vietnam are held by women, compared to the global average of 19 per cent. Women's membership in the Communist Party has also risen from over 20 per cent in 2005 to more than 30 per cent in 2010 (UNDP, 2014). The high proportion of female-led businesses across company ownership types was evident in this study's participants. About two-thirds of our interviewees were women managers or business owners.

The above historical background of Vietnam indicates a strong emphasis on Vietnamese national identity, as well as a blending of traditional culture and socialist ideology (Collins 2009; Edwards and Phan, 2013). Traditional thinkers, such as Confucius, have also had an influence on the management of Vietnam (e.g. Warner, 2013).

At the societal level, the gradualist approach noted above towards transition has led to a diversified economy and, in turn, to the 'fusion' of different ideologies and cultural values – including Confucianism, socialism and 'capitalism – with Vietnamese characteristics' (Collins, 2009). The stereotypical view of paternalistic leadership does not necessary capture the richness and complexity involved in everyday realities where managers have to cope with a range of different, complementary and sometimes antagonistic sociocultural influences (Ren et al., 2014). Despite the tensions managers experience in balancing economic and social goals in their work, their priorities at the individual level still appear to be determined by the enduring influence of their societal culture. Therefore, the continued transitional stage reflected in the perceptions and practices of leadership may be best understood from the locally rooted cultural perspective of Vietnamese managers, rather than Western-derived models (Edwards and Phan, 2013).

When the theme of leadership was introduced into our interviews, both the English word 'leadership' and the Vietnamese equivalent *lãnh đạo* were used whenever possible in order to confirm that participants were discussing the central concept of the research. Findings from primary data show that the majority of participants commented on the distinction between being a manager and being a leader, with the former entailing the application of organizational structures and rules, whereas the latter was perceived to mean 'getting things done in the right way'. However, the 'devil is always in the detail', as we shall shortly see.

All respondents from SOEs believed that in order to work successfully as a manager, one should also be a good leader who takes extra care of one's employees. The respondents saw employees as their family members. As leaders, they indicated that they needed to make the right moral decisions; that was important for both the company's long-term reputation and for individual employees. For leadership to succeed, all participants of SOEs and DPEs – regardless of their firm ownership, tenure, gender, age or qualification – believed in 'following the local role-models', 'setting a good example' and 'upholding moral standards'. To be a good business leader in the current market economy, Vietnamese managers need to have all three ingredients, as well as moral obligations to employees, ethical and social awareness, and high managerial skills or field knowledge. Among these three important items, moral obligation is the most important.

Influence of foreign management practices

Transition towards market-oriented economies has indeed generated many changing cultural values, competing demands and diverse expectations related to leadership, a context perhaps somewhat more complex than in established economies (Warner et al., 2005; Collins et al., 2013; Rowley and Ulrich, 2014). New ways of doing things have diffused in Vietnam (*Phong cách làm việc hiện đại*), via Chinese Confucian traditionalism in past times, French colonialism in the 19th century, Soviet assistance to the North and US aid to the South after the middle of the 20th century, among others (Warner, 2013). Since the end of the 'Vietnam War', the newly re-unified nation embarked on its journey from a traditional socialist economy to a market-oriented one (although still 'Marxist' in name) in the 1980s. As a result of the economic reforms, Vietnam has shown sustainable economic achievements, assisted also by the encouragement of foreign direct investment (FDI) in the country through its friendly Foreign Investment Law passed in 1987 (Collins and Zhu, 2005). This new form of business has gradually changed the corporate landscape, moving it from being dominated by SOEs to becoming a multi-sector economy. It has shifted the country's people-management systems over recent years, from what was previously known as Personnel Management (PM) to the newer Human Resource Management (HRM) introduced by the FDI sector since the start of economic reform; expressed in Vietnamese, PM (*quản lý nhân sự*) has given way to HRM (*quản lý nguồn nhân lực*) (Collins, et al., 2011, Warner, 2013). Effective management in FDI businesses in Vietnam has spread through to local businesses. Today this new model depends increasingly on managers, be they men or women, within these companies being willing to undertake leadership roles (*vai trò lãnh đạo*) and fulfil the expectations of employees, whether explicitly or implicitly (Cox et al., 2014; Liu et al., 2003).

The focus of this study is the theoretical and practical consideration of the determinants of leadership effectiveness (*hiệu quả lãnh đạo*). More than ever leadership (*khả năng lãnh đạo*) remains an important issue in Vietnam's businesses. Despite the foregoing reforms aimed at nurturing market-oriented mechanisms – such as the establishment of the 'employment contract system' (*chế độ hợp đồng lao động*) and elimination of the 'jobs for life' (*biên chế*) system in the SOEs – preserving the Communist Party's leadership is said to still remain a priority (Collins and Zhu, 2005; Collins et al., 2011). In order to preserve order, the government is prepared to negotiate with enterprises and make compromises if the reforms or imported ideas go too far and are not amenable to what is required in the Party's eyes (Collins, 2009; Collins et al., 2011). Although many changes have taken place in business operations and practices, it would appear that a 'harmonious' and 'cooperative' relationship based on indigenous values is still pervasive, regardless of the ownership of the organization.

The influence of foreign management practices is also reflected in differences among SOEs, DPEs and FOEs, being more evident in areas related to how to engage with employees and approach ethical issues. Most of the interviewees indicated that they felt pressure to engage with their employees through effective communications, and this pressure was more acute in domestic enterprises (i.e. SOEs and DPEs). The need for employee engagement is partly due to the changing workforce, where new generations have entered the labour market and expressed interest in being included in the operation and decision-making process. Many employees favour a leader who makes an effort to communicate with them frequently. Such communications make employees feel they are valued and included at work. This helps to build their willingness to cooperate with leaders and with each other. This could be seen as gradually adopting certain elements of transformational leadership.

The above observation was echoed by interviewees from other DPEs and SOEs in our study. Unlike FOEs, where HRM systems are relatively well established, the communication channels in these domestic enterprises were often seen as ambiguous and nominal in nature. Our interviewees in DPEs were sometimes frustrated and doubted whether they understood their employees, who were a mixture of different generations and mindsets. To be seen as an effective leader in DPEs, the managers felt that they needed to 'do extra' and nurture relationships with employees not only at work but also outside working hours. These managers were normally involved in outside business activities with their employees – such attending weddings, birthday parties or funerals of employees' family members, or sponsoring scholarships for employee's children. Some managers of DPEs had experience of working for SOEs previously and found these outside activities were necessary for establishing good communications and understanding with employees, in turn leading to good management practices. Many DPE participants revealed that they saw a great need to update their skills and knowledge to keep up with the fast changes in business. However, they also stated that 'self-learning' (*tu hoc*) to improve or update their knowledge on new management approaches or tools was most common due to the lack of a formal degree or courses for leadership development.

According to participants from this sector, two key areas would need to be updated: industrial technical skills and management skills. While the older participants think that following traditional practices is crucial, the younger managers commonly think they need to update their skills and knowledge to keep up with fast changes in their sectors, as well as to understand other sectors' practices. Many of these younger managers enrol part time in MBA evening courses, but find that these courses are designed for standard business practices which are often not related to the Vietnamese businesses environment, or are not practical enough. However, attending MBA courses is still thought to help provide some theoretical basis to understand Western models of management, in the hope that this knowledge will be of assistance at a later stage.

Another key difference between participants in our study is the approach towards ethics and morality. Eight interviewees from the FOEs studied indicated that business operations and practices are largely transferred from their MNCs' Western headquarters or counterpart companies with better-established HRM systems rather than domestic companies. A management leader here is expected to practise 'ethical leadership' and be a role model; however, this relates mainly to simply following the organizational rules and industry codes of conduct. Interestingly, 9 out of 12 FOE respondents placed as much importance on the technical/management skills of leaders as on moral and ethical aspects, while the majority of domestic company respondents (25) thought the moral or ethical aspects were of the highest importance in leaders. In domestic companies, paternalism continues to underpin expectations imposed on a leader to behave 'ethically' and practise 'virtues'. In DPEs, a leader is expected to practise virtues to overcome challenges arising from a lack of resources. In SOEs, given that bureaucratic inertia remains evident, a leader wields authoritarian power and influences subordinates through 'personal virtue'. As mentioned earlier, respondents from SOEs saw themselves as 'parents' in their collective working environment. There was a clear hierarchy in this context, but friendly and open communications, allowing leaders to treat their employees as their own family members. This was different with FOEs, where leaders also practised 'ethical' behaviours but did not feel the need to treat employees as family. These leaders needed to act ethically toward their employees to gain their trust; but, more importantly, the leaders needed to have excellent field knowledge to impress their employees and lead them in their day-to-day work. They did not see themselves as their employees' family members, and believed in dealing with work-related matters according to company rules. The managers believed in very strong market competition and that they needed to maintain a good balance between being a friend and being a leader. Managers from the FOEs interviewed identified an excess of outdated practices that held back business operations and relied too heavily on personal relationships. Therefore, it is evident that the FDI sector is in favour of a greater degree of law and order in the workplace to achieve 'best practices'. However, there is also an awareness that managers cannot simply act according to law and order in the context of Vietnam; a good balance between a friendly (ethical) and well-ordered working environment will achieve the goal of creating harmony in the workplace.

Tension

Most Asian management research, including research on Vietnam, draws heavily on established Western theories. While we acknowledge the merits of such approaches, we will argue that the theorization of leadership in Vietnam requires a more nuanced acknowledgement that the nature of human thought differs there, as opposed to in the West, in so far as it manifests itself as different behavioural responses (Peterson and Wood, 2008). Specifically, the belief system and cognitive process prevalent in many East Asian countries are characterized by a more holistic, contradictory and interrelated view of the world than in typical Western countries. Influenced by Confucianism, among a number of philosophies, the collective and interdependent tradition leads to a consideration of a host of factors operating with each other in a more complex and sometimes elusive way (Ren et al., 2014). The doctrine of 'harmony' and 'balance' may thus lead to an appreciation of 'contradictions' and 'flux'. Emphasis on 'ways of living' may contribute to the tendency of 'doing', rather than a search for absolute truth and a dependency on scientific theory (Nisbett, 2003; Hofstede, 2001).

Whilst Western-inspired research on Vietnam has surged since the mid-2000s (e.g. Zhu et al., 2008; Rowley and Truong, 2009; Rowley and Vo, 2010; Rowley et al., 2010), scholarly literature focusing on an indigenous paradigm of effective leader-performance (*thực hành lãnh đạo có hiệu quả*) remains relatively scarce. Under these circumstances, the simple transfer of Western concepts, models and theories may well be problematic because it may overlook constructs and phenomena salient to a different context shaped by specific traditional legacy, cultural history and institutional forces (e.g. Nisbett, 2003; Child, 2009; Leung, 2009; Collins and Chou, 2013; Collins et al., 2014).

Findings from FOE participants show that despite exposure to Western cultures and the *Đổi mới* reforms, the working motto was adopted from the principles of Communist leader Hồ Chí Minh. These principles, as also commented on by most of the Vietnamese interviewees, involved (at least *prima facie*) the endorsement of Communist ideology (such as 'Party control', 'egalitarianism' and 'serving the people wholeheartedly') and traditional values (such as 'contributing to the collective good' and 'maintaining belongingness as a whole'). We found that there was broad agreement among almost all respondents that for a Vietnamese leader to be 'effective' the leader must lead through 'orientation towards harmony'. This condition firstly requires a sacrifice of personal time and effort, which was indicated in the case of most respondents from FOEs – who commonly held Western post-graduate qualifications and may even have had experience of working and living in Western countries. These respondents found that being a manager in the US differed from being a manager in Vietnam.

The respondents believed that leaders should set a good example for everyone to follow. Creating a harmonious and healthy workplace and avoiding conflict at all costs are among the key duties of leaders. Managers in

FOEs agreed that they had learned most of the technical skills used in their job through their overseas training, but that they only learned how to be a good leader when they combined their Western practices with their Vietnamese traditional culture of leadership. Overtime, for example, is a common practice in Vietnam, and the issue of 'work–life balance' is largely ignored. One FOE manager explained the motive behind this phenomenon with the slogan 'to expect a great career, one needs a strong spirit' (*Muốn nên sự nghiệp lớn, tinh thần cần phải cao*). For all of our interviewees (40), 'self-sacrifice' was generated, on the one hand, by a strong belief in persistence and, on the other hand, by the social expectation to be successful.

Furthermore, interviewees claimed that 'harmony' is achieved through the realization of 'common goals'. Out of 40 participants, 35 also commented on the 'realization of common goals' as an important outcome of effective leadership. In the case of SOEs, although the traditional perception of 'regarding the company as family' was no longer dominant in younger-generation leaders, a 'win–win' mindset was still pervasive. In the DPEs and FOEs studied, most (24) respondents also tended to align management outcomes with the interests of potential stakeholders. The benefits of such a practice included 'enhancing people's faith in their work', 'motivating people', 'building trust' and 'maintaining relationships in the long run'. We also found evidence of the stronger traditional culture of Confucianism in Vietnamese business culture, which is to a certain degree consistent with key elements of transformational leadership and authentic leadership in the West.

The above practices have a great impact on employees' expectations of their managers and leaders today, whether in SOEs, DPEs or FOEs. A leader in a firm needs to learn how to motivate employees by creating a friendly working environment rather than a competitive one. Friday lunches or dinners for employees are common events held to build trust and harmony among stakeholders.

Additionally, most (30) Vietnamese participants still saw their leaders as being paternalistic, due to the responsibilities related to contributing to the collective values regardless of ownership type. For example, most of the participants stated that their companies still provided a range of free lunch options because they believed that organizational well-being goes hand in hand with individual well-being. These businesses do not focus solely on profits, but rather endeavour to benefit the community of workers. Only by promoting a harmonious and moral environment can leaders make employees happy, and these will then become motivated to work for the company.

Leadership development programmes in Vietnam

The Global Talent Competitiveness Index (GTCI) is an annual benchmarking report that measures the ability of countries to compete for talent. The report ranks over 100 countries according to their ability to grow, attract and retain talent. The GTCI combines the academic research and expertise of INSEAD, an international business school, and Singapore's Human Capital Leadership Institute (HCLI) with the business experience and perspective of Adecco, a world leader in HR solutions. According to the 2015–2016 report, Vietnam ranks 82 out of 109 countries and territories, compared to a rank of 75 in 2014–2015 (a drop of seven places). The gap between Vietnam and other countries in Southeast Asia such as Singapore, Malaysia, the Philippines and Thailand in the rankings is substantial. Specifically, the 2015–2016 report shows that Malaysia is ranked No. 30, the Philippines 56, Thailand 69 and Singapore No. 2. Within the Association of Southeast Asian Nations (ASEAN), Vietnam is ranked above Cambodia (No. 96) and Indonesia (No. 90). Vietnam was ranked higher for Global Knowledge (using high skills to support initiatives and engage in business) and lower in the Labour and Vocational category, as well as in the category of attracting, developing and retaining talent. Although Vietnam's performance was seen as poor in developing talent through the formal education system, it achieved a high score in Global Knowledge (above Thailand). According to the report, the biggest gap between Vietnam and leading countries is in the Labour and Vocational area. Vietnam was ranked low for its ability to attract and develop talent, and for its Sustainability and Life Style capability. The report also shows that Vietnam's points for Innovation and Entrepreneurship were high. However, Vietnam faces the risk of losing existing talent, which can hinder the growth of the economy (ASEAN, 2016).

In terms of local institutes providing business leadership training, there has been growth in the number of MBA programmes in Vietnam since 2000. The programmes vary in ownership and design to fit different cohorts of students and learners. The top four programmes are currently run by: the Royal Melbourne Institute of Technology (RMIT); Management Institute FSB/FPT University; Centre Franco-Vietnamien de formation à la Gestion (CFVG); and the University of Economics Ho Chi Minh City (UEH).

RMIT is an Australian-based university operating in Vietnam, with campuses in Ho Chi Minh City and Hanoi. The Vietnamese branch is officially known as RMIT University Vietnam and its Australian counterpart is known as RMIT University. RMIT Vietnam was officially founded in 2001 and commenced offering courses at its purpose-built campus in Ho Chi Minh City. Until 2016 it was the only wholly foreign-owned university in Vietnam which provided MBAs identical to its Melbourne counterpart. RMIT Vietnam offers three options at both campuses: Master of Business Administration (MBA), Executive Master of Business Administration (EMBA) and Master of International Business (MIB). These can be taken in a one year, full-time accelerated mode or as part-time study for working students. The university has been awarded 10 Golden Dragon Awards for its 'excellence in education' by the Vietnamese Ministry of Trade since 2003. It has also been rewarded by the Australian Chamber of Commerce for its 'innovation and community service', and has received Certificates of Merit from the Ho Chi Minh City People's Committee and the Hanoi Government. In 2008, RMIT

International University received a Certificate of Merit from the Prime Minister of Vietnam, Nguyen Tan Dung, for its 'educational achievements contributing to the social and economic development of Vietnam'.[1]

Management Institute FSB, founded in 2006 and owned by FPT University, was the first private university in Vietnam. FPT University is a member of the information technology multinational FPT Vietnam Group. FSB's MBA programme has run for 13 years and started its collaborative programme with the UK's University of Greenwich in 2009. Today FSB is well known in Vietnam, and its MBA has achieved five awards from QS Star.[2]

CFVG is a joint project in management education signed in 1992 by the French Ministry of Foreign Affairs and the Vietnamese Ministry of Education and Training. It is operated by CCI Paris Ile-de-France, which boasts the largest network of business schools and teaching resources in Europe. CFVG has collaborated in Vietnam with the National Economics University and University of Economics Ho Chi Minh City. All courses at CFVG are taught in English and French. Currently the centre has about 600 postgraduate students.[3]

The University of Economics Ho Chi Minh City (UEH) was established in 1976. It is one of the 15 key national universities of Vietnam and is a member of the Best 1000 Business Schools in the World. UEH has been a renowned centre of scientific research, providing undergraduate and postgraduate education for students from Vietnam and neighbouring Laos and Cambodia. In 2010 UEH opened the International School of Business (ISB) as an English-speaking school to offer undergraduate and postgraduate courses in business, business administration, public administration and finance. At postgraduate level, ISB provides a large range of degrees such as WSU MBA, Executive MBA, Master of Finance MFIN, Master of Business MBUS and Master of Public Administration MPA. All courses are taught in English and follow an international academic format. The ISB has a partnership with the University of Western Sydney, as well as associations with Victoria University in Australia, Université du Québec à Montréal (UQAM) in Canada and the University of Houston-Clear Lake, USA.[4]

Evaluation and conclusion

In recent years, business leaders in the Asian transitional economies have become the subject of diverse disciplines, particularly as an attempt to understand the strength of their economic achievements when growth elsewhere has largely slowed down (Edwards and Phan, 2013). These leaders constitute an essential part of the driving force of the rapid expansion of such economies. Our interpretation of the data collected from this study provides clear empirical support for a 'context-specific', indigenous explanation grounded in the ongoing economic transition and societal transformation processes to be found in Vietnam. A general pattern emerges from our analysis indicating that effective leadership performance in Vietnam is even more complex since it entails a holistic approach emphasizing the appropriate handling of the intricacies of contacts, networks and relationships. This supersedes the points frequently emphasized in the contractual governance approach concerning the performance of clearly defined roles, and moves onto another plane using what has been called a 'relational epistemology', as reflected in the mode of logic and way of thinking involved therein (Nisbett, 2003).

The view that the nature of social structure is collective and interdependent has interpreted leadership in this context as having an orientation towards common goals and best outcomes for the interests of the collective group. As this study implies, people are not rewarded, or even penalized through isolation or a damaged reputation, should they disturb such a balance. Achieving coherence through common goals suggests a relational perspective, focusing on 'win-win' solutions. While holistic and relationship-oriented leadership is not new to Western managers, this research has aimed to add meaning and substance to this observation in the new context of Vietnam. The transitional context has produced a range of paradoxes for managers to understand and according to which they should behave; in particular, managers have to cope with a mix of changing cultural values. Market-based competition for profits and self-interest has made its way into the minds and life of Vietnamese business leaders, though at a different pace. Nonetheless, the far-reaching tradition of social equilibrium through harmony has much contemporary relevance. This study also shows a strong paradoxical belief in traditional Confucian values, alongside Communist ideology. These managers adhere to the long-standing tradition of suppressing personal interests, with emphasis placed primarily on the interests of the public, including people, work-units and society at large. As far as contradictions and irony in the interviewees' 'real-life' responses are concerned, the researchers remain cautious in interpreting any inconsistencies.

The results of this study have presented the differences between traditional and modern leadership styles among Vietnamese managers, as well as high degrees of adaptation to local context in foreign companies doing business in Vietnam. The leadership practices of indigenous firms in Vietnam are also influenced by the presence of an increasing number of multinationals (MNCs), where FOEs seem to influence and set minimum standards in terms of management practices.

In conclusion, this study explores leadership in Vietnam through meaningful contextualization. Results of the study illustrate how ongoing economic transition and societal transformation influence the evaluation of leader performance and style. On the one hand, the prevalence of Vietnam's traditional legacy conveys a holistic approach towards leader performance beyond the contractual governance approach concerning the performance of clearly defined roles. On the other hand, this study shows the interaction and sometimes tension between traditional legacy and Western influence during the process of transition. By highlighting the differences found in SOEs, DPEs and FOEs, this study describes the process of change in business leadership among Vietnam's companies and how the context of this transitional economy has influenced the adaptation vis-à-vis standardization of business leadership practices in modern Vietnam. This study has highlighted certain aspects of Vietnam's business leadership. First, motivation to learn and develop has long been widely pervasive in Vietnam, and is captured in the old Vietnamese saying that 'the book is not the last page' (*Sự học là cuốn sách không trang cuối cùng*). There is also evidence of 'paternalistic leadership' (Chao and Kao, 2005; Chen and Kao, 2009; Farh and Cheng, 2000). Such leadership may combine authoritarianism with fatherly benevolence and moral integrity (Cheng et al., 2000). A paternalistic leader is said to be expected to act as a model equivalent to a 'parent' and to treat employees as their children, particularly in Asia. The underlying cultural roots reinforce this patriarchal historical tradition in which a leader has the legitimate right to exercise power, closely monitor subordinates and make final decisions in the interest of others. However, times may be changing as a new generation takes over. Finally, there is a great demand for suitable leadership development of current business leaders, especially in the DPE sector, which seems to have less formal structures of management but is a faster growing sector compared with SOEs and FDIs.

Furthermore, continued economic reforms and industrial transformation have influenced leadership concepts to form and reform in ways that are found in Vietnam but are not yet fully understood. These concepts are far from being embedded in mainstream leadership theories, and consequently need further future study.

Notes

1 www.rmit.edu.vn/postgraduate-programs.
2 http://mba.fsb.edu.vn.
3 www.cfvg.org.
4 www.isb.edu.vn.

References

ASEAN (2016) 'Vietnam: Vietnam falls in ranking in Global Talent Competitiveness Index', https://search.proquest.com/docview/1765706773?accountid=13552 [accessed on 20 April 2017].

BBC (2016) 'The Vietnamese women who fought for their country', www.bbc.com/news/in-pictures-37986986 [accessed on 26 April 2017].

Chao, A.A. and Kao, S.R. (2005) 'Paternalistic leadership and subordinated stress in Taiwanese enterprises', *Research in Applied Psychology*, 27(1): 111–131.

Chen, H.-Y. and Kao, H.S.-R. (2009) 'Chinese paternalistic leadership and non-Chinese subordinates psychological health', *International Journal of Human Resource Management*, 20(12): 2533–2546.

Cheng, B.S., Chou, L.F. and Farh, J.L. (2000) 'A triad model of paternalistic leadership: Constructs and measurement', *Indigenous Psychological Research in Chinese Societies*, 14(1): 3–64.

Chi, K. and Trang, T. (2016) 'Role of Vietnamese women changing', *Vietnam News*, 7 March, http://vietnamnews.vn/print/role-of-vietnamese-women-changing/283270.html [accessed on 26 April 2017].

Child, J. (2009) 'Context, comparison, and methodology in Chinese management research', *Management and Organization Review*, 5(1): 57–73.

Collins, N. (2009) *Economic Reform and Employment Relations in Vietnam*, London and New York: Routledge.

Collins, N. (2011) 'Vietnam's labour relations and global financial crisis', *Research and Practice Human Resource Management*, 19(2), 60–70.

Collins, N. and Chou, Y. (2013) 'Building team trust: A study in the Asian context', *Journal of American Business Review, Cambridge*, 1(2): 181–188.

Collins, N. and Zhu, Y. (2005) 'The transformation of HRM in transitional Economies: The case of Vietnam', *Journal of Comparative Asian Development*, 4(1): 161–178.

Collins, N., Chou, Y. and Warner, M. (2014) 'Member satisfaction, communication and role of leader in virtual self-managed teamwork: Case-studies in Asia-Pacific region', *Human Systems Management*, 33(3):155–170.

Collins, N., Zhu, Y. and Warner, M. (2012) 'HRM and Asian economies in transition: China Vietnam and North Korea', in C. Brewster and W. Wolfgang Mayrhofer (eds), *Handbook of Research in Comparative Human Resource Management*, Cheltenham: Edward Elgar, pp. 577–598.

Collins, N., Sitalaksmi, S. and Lansbury, R. (2013) 'Transforming employment relations in Vietnam and Indonesia: Case-studies of state-owned enterprises', *Asia Pacific Journal of Human Resources*, 51: 131–151.

Collins, N., Nankervis, A., Sitalaksmi, S. and Warner, M. (2011) 'Labour–management relationships in transitional economies: Convergence or divergence in Vietnam and Indonesia?', *Asia Pacific Business Review*, 17(3): 316–377.

Cox, A., Hannif, Z. and Rowley, C. (2014) 'Leadership styles and generational effects: examples of US companies in Vietnam', *International Journal of Human Resources Management*, 25(1): 1–22.

Economist Intelligence Unit (2015) 'Update: Vietnam',http://country.eiu.com/vietnam [accessed on 20 April 2014].

Edwards, V. and Phan, A. (2013) *Managers and Management in Vietnam: 25 Years of Economic Renovation (Đổi mới)*, London and New York: Routledge.

Farh, J. L. and Cheng, G. S. (2000) 'A cultural analysis of paternalistic leadership in Chinese organizations', in J.T. Li, A.S. Tsui and E. Weldon (eds), *Management and Organizations in the Chinese Context*, Basingstoke: Macmillan, pp. 84–127.

Fforde, A. (2007) *Vietnamese State Industry and the Political Economy of Commercial Renaissance: Dragon's Tooth or Curate's Egg?* Oxford: Chandos.

Hofstede, G. (2001) *Culture's Consequences: Comparing Values, Behaviors, Institutions, and Organizations across Nations* (2nd edition), Thousand Oaks, CA: Sage.

Hong, A. (2016) 'Vietnam elects first female legislature leader', *Vietnam Express International*, 31 March, http://e.vnexpress.net/news/news/vietnam-elects-first-female-legislature-leader-3378891.html [accessed on 26 April 2017].

Leung, K. (2009) 'Never the twain shall meet? Integrating Chinese and Western management research', *Management and Organization Review*, 5(1): 121–129.

Leung, S. (2015) 'The Vietnamese economy: Seven years after the global financial crisis', *Journal of Southeast Asian Economies*, 32(1): 1–10.

Liu, W., Lepak, D.P., Takeuchi, R. and Sims, H.P. (2003) 'Matching leadership styles with employment modes: strategic human resource management perspective', *Human Resource Management Review*, 13(1): 127–152.

Nguyen, T.N., Mort, G.S. and D'Souza, C. (2015) 'Vietnam in transition: SMEs and the necessitating environment for entrepreneurship development', *Entrepreneurship & Regional Development: An International Journal*, 27: 154–180.

Nguyen, T. N., Truong, Q. and Buyens, D. (2011) 'Training and firm performance in economies in transition: A comparison between Vietnam and China', *Asia Pacific Business Review*, 17(1): 103–119.

Nisbett, R.E. (2003) *The Geography of Thought: How Asians and Westerners Think Differently … and Why*, New York: Free Press.

Peterson, M.F. and Wood, R.E. (2008) 'Cognitive structures and processes in cross-cultural management', in P.B. Smith, M.F. Peterson and R. E. Wood (eds), *Handbook of Cross-Cultural Management Research*, Thousand Oaks, CA: Sage, pp. 15–33.

Reese, L. (2016) 'The Trung Sisters', Women in World History Curriculum, www.wom eninworldhistory.com/heroine10.html [accessed on 24 April 2017].

Ren, S., Collins, N. and Zhu, Y. (2014) 'Self-development of leadership competencies in China and Vietnam', *Asia Pacific Journal of Human Resources*, 52: 42–59.

Rowley, C. and Truong, Q. (2009) *The Changing Face of Vietnamese Management*, London and New York: Routledge.

Rowley, C. and Ulrich, D. (2014) *Leadership in the Asia Pacific: A Global Research Perspective*, London and New York: Routledge.

Rowley, C. and Vo, A. (2010) 'The internationalisation of IR? Japanese and US MNCs in Vietnam', *Asia Pacific Business Review*, 16(1): 221–238.

Rowley, C., Truong, Q. and Van der Heijden, B. (2010) 'Globalisation, competitiveness and HRM in transitional economy: Vietnam', *International Journal of Business Studies*, 18(1): 75–100.

Truong, H.T. (2008) 'Women's leadership in Vietnam: Opportunities and challenges', *Signs: Journal of Women in Culture and Society*, 34(1):16–21.

UNDP (2014) *Women's Leadership in Vietnam: Leveraging a Resource Untapped*, www.undp.org/content/dam/vietnam/docs/Publications/Women%20Leadership%20in% 20Viet%20Nam%20Leveraging%20A%20Resource%20Untapped.pdfeterson [accessed on 26 April 2017].

Warner, M. (2013) 'Comparing human resource management in China and Vietnam: An overview', *Human Systems Management*, 32(2): 217–229.

Warner, M., Edwards, V., Polonsky, G., Pučko, D. and Zhu, Y. (2005) *Management in Transitional Economies: From the Berlin Wall to the Great Wall of China*, London and New York: Routledge Curzon.

Zhu, Y., Collins, N., Webber, M., and Benson, J. (2008) 'New forms of ownership and human resource practices in Vietnam', *Human Resource Management*, 47(1): 157–175.

9 Conclusion

Comparative analysis of business leaders and leadership in Asia

Introduction

This book has addressed complex issues relating to business leaders and leadership in Asia vis-à-vis underpinning theories and contextual background using six Asian economies as case studies. The purpose was to provide a holistic analysis of a wide range of influencing factors – in philosophical, historical, cultural, social, political and economic domains – that form and shape business leaders and leadership in Asia. This book also endeavours to enrich understandings of management/leadership theories and practices in the East and the West.

At the beginning of the book we developed a number of key research questions that guided the design of each case study chapter. In this concluding chapter, we start our discussion by summarizing the overall responses to these questions based on the findings of the case studies. By doing so, we present a general comparative analysis of the key characteristics of business leaders and leadership among the six Asian economies studied, which in turn will allow us to identify different patterns or models on the subject. Based on these patterns, we further develop a general comparative platform with a number of important characteristics that distinguish business leaders and leadership in the East and the West. Finally, the closing section highlights the major challenges for further development of research and practices of business leaders and leadership not only in Asia, but also globally.

Responding to the key questions

In Chapter 2, we developed three key questions, namely:

- What are the traditional values and thinking influencing management and leadership practices?
- What has changed in terms of leadership concepts and practices influenced by 'Western' concepts under the process of globalization?
- What are the key concerns of business leaders in East Asia in confronting challenges and becoming successful and sustainable leaders?

The first key objective of this concluding chapter is to address these issues.

We observed the deep-rooted impact of traditional values and thinking on leaders' management and leadership practices, particularly from Confucianism (Table 9.1). Paternalistic leadership is one of the key characteristics of East Asian leadership style, with an emphasis on authoritarian rule as well as an ordered and, ideally, benevolent social hierarchy. Consistent with Confucian doctrine, a good leader is seen as a good parent, with power but also showing kindness toward subordinates, setting a good example of moral standards for others to follow. In difficult times, a good leader sacrifices self-interest. The ideal paternalistic leader maintains a balance between authoritarian control and benevolence (Rindova and Starbuck, 1997).

However, many examples presented in some of the chapters indicate that with increasing economic pressure in general, and a certain historical impact in particular (e.g. military training background of leaders in certain economies under a political dictatorship regime), many business leaders may adopt more authoritarian-oriented leadership without balancing it with benevolent behaviour. In reality, it is much easier for leaders to exercise control with power, but less so to present themselves as kind and benevolent. In addition, the authoritarian style of leadership is further reinforced by other underpinning philosophical views such as Legalism, which emphasizes 'control by rule' and punishment (Watson, 1964).

The co-existence of benevolence-related and authoritarian-oriented leadership styles reflects a balanced view that is prevalent in most Asian countries, again consistent with 'the doctrine of means' (*zhongyong*) upheld by Confucius. In addition, a balanced approach to issues is also a key tenet of the concept of *Yin* and *Yang*, which is influential in efforts to be adaptable and flexible.

As for the other traditional schools of thought, the so-called 'effortless' approach towards leaders and leadership advocated by both Daoism and Confucianism (though in different ways) has not been adopted widely among business leaders in Asia. This may be due to the reality that these leaders have predominately a mentality of control and consciously manage as leaders, an act which cannot in itself be effortless or devoid of control.

From this perspective, we can see that reality reflects a more complex leadership style. There are signs of following traditional values and thinking, but other factors – such as historical background, political system and engagement with the international economy – are also involved in the process of shaping leadership styles. An interesting phenomenon in engagement with the international economy is represented by the actions of foreign MNCs, which bring transactional-oriented thinking and practices into East Asian economies, making paternalistic leadership in East Asia even more results-driven and authoritarian-oriented. We have observed this in a number of economies in East Asia, including China and Vietnam, after their economic reforms.

With regard to the second question – namely the influence of 'Western' concepts of leadership in East Asia – we observed variations in the historical,

Table 9.1 Comparison of key issues of business leaders and leadership among six case studies

Case	Value/thinking and leadership	Western/foreign influence on leadership	Key tensions and concerns of business leaders
Japan	Confucianism/Shinto/Zen Buddhism: enlightenment/virtuous behaviour harmony/collectivism social order/hierarchy accepting current social status strong spirit of 'tinkerer'.	Transformational leadership more than transactional leadership (i.e. relational and humanistic value).	Tension between established Japanese practices and Western practices (i.e. the impact of business internationalization).
		More emphasis on situational and authentic leadership recently.	Mixed business leadership styles (i.e. to cope with constant changes).
	Leadership: paternalism/benevolence/moral example (mendou) authority vs. autonomy (omakase) hierarchy/personal loyalty wa – horizontal harmony (but not vertical) collectivism/common goal/uniformity social network risk avoidance.	Introducing '3-self': - self-motivation - self-management - self-awareness.	Women's leadership is a challenging issue.
			More tolerant towards failure among new economic sectors.
		Adopting rational business practices incorporate into Japanese business methods.	Developing new company culture by combining old and new elements.
			Employees as agent of change.
			In sum, pragmatic evolution with constant adjustment.

Case	Value/thinking and leadership	Western/foreign influence on leadership	Key tensions and concerns of business leaders
South Korea	Confucianism/Buddhism: social order based on hierarchy, collectivism emphasis on humility, personal virtue and enlightenment. Leadership: paternalism/autocratic/group-oriented authoritarian leadership based on hierarchy and seniority personal virtue with diligence vertical and horizontal harmony (inhwa) with empathy interaction with subordinate beyond work domains/long-term relationship higher level of acceptance of risks and innovation leaders of big corporations developing and maintaining close relationship with government personal relationship building for leaders of small companies.	Strong influence of US and Japanese business management and leadership practices. Adopting effective leadership with frequent changes of leaders based on performance and results More emphasis recently on transformational leadership style with openness, participation, sharing and consensus building.	Traditional social network vs. nepotism. Low level of women's leadership. Limited institutional and social support for women leaders. Conscription engenders hierarchy, results-orientation and competition within developing leadership competencies. Business leader development focuses on individual performance and competence by linking training, promotion and career development. Transforming the norm of personal virtue with diligence to organizational based ethical conduct and behaviour.

Case	Value/thinking and leadership	Western/foreign influence on leadership	Key tensions and concerns of business leaders
Taiwan	Confucianism/Daoism/Yijing/Legalism/Buddhism: social order based on hierarchy, collectivism, personal virtue and enlightenment importance of the balanced way (*Yin* and *Yang*) or the mid-way (*zhongyong*). Leadership: paternalistic – combining benevolence, morality, authoritarianism and charisma face culture influences on *guanxi* network and reciprocity relationship building 'tinkerer' behaviour of high commitment, paying attention to details, and continuing improvement value-based with self-sacrifice.	Strong influence of US and Japanese business management and leadership practices. Adopting charismatic leadership, transformational leadership, ethical and virtue leadership by combining with certain elements of 'new model' of paternalistic leadership.	A leader with special capability provides a vision that emphasizes reciprocity and meets the need of social transformation. The new combination model based on charismatic leadership, paternalistic leadership and moral/ethical leadership has an incremental effect; such a leadership style is better received by subordinates and leads to greater satisfaction. Transformational leadership also adds value on inspirational motivation, individualized consideration and intellectual stimulation to subordinates. Women leadership is improving. Transforming from 'rule of man' to 'rule of law'. Adopting the situational leadership concept in order to bring success and flexibility to business. Adoptive leaders need to develop the habit of ongoing learning through self-development.

Case	Value/thinking and leadership	Western/foreign influence on leadership	Key tensions and concerns of business leaders
Singapore	Confucianism rooted in the Chinese business communities, plus British colonial rule-influenced modern business/management thinking and practices. Strong government influences on businesses/management. Leadership: paternalistic leadership style mixed with Western transactional leadership balanced approach towards short-term and long-term goals hard-working behaviour/self-sacrifice vigilant on business opportunities capacity to overcome great difficulties integration of Eastern (e.g. win–win mindset, social network) and Western ways (e.g. contractual obligation, economic rationalism over resources control and allocation).	Earlier influence was based on British colonial rule; emphasis on economic rationalism and transaction, hence transactional leadership style was a dominating leadership phenomenon. Increasing MNCs' regional headquarters influence management and leadership practices by introducing all kind of best practice, hence leadership shifts towards transformational, interactive, instructional, situational, ethical and authentic leadership styles.	Tensions between traditional leadership styles and practices and new concepts and practices brought by foreign MNCs. Too dependent on government protection and support; reluctant to be involved in overseas business operation on their own. Concerns about continuing improvement of competitiveness given increasing regional-based competition from other Asian economies. Women's leadership is improving but still has gaps and difficulties. Effective development for young leadership is critical and requires more innovative, confident combining with formal training programmes

Case	Value/thinking and leadership	Western/foreign influence on leadership	Key tensions and concerns of business leaders
China	Combination of traditional values (e.g. Confucianism, Daoism, Yijing, Legalism, Buddhism) with recent influences of nationalism, communism and market economic reform. Leadership: authoritarianism with hierarchy paternalism common goals and 'self-sacrifice' face culture, reciprocity and *guanxi* network vertical and horizontal harmony a mid-way.	Since economic reform and 'open door policy', transactional leadership has taken the importance. Nonetheless gradually transformational leadership, servant leadership, authentic leadership, empowering leadership, have become more important. Adoption of different leadership styles is contingent upon firm ownership structure. The meaning of ethical leadership differs in China and in US.	Business leaders with global mindsets, especially related to engaging with overseas operations at the higher end of the value chain. Increasing entrepreneurial spirit while searching for inspirational role models with ability to navigate China's further reform and transformation. Much higher proportion of women leaders than in other Asian economies. Ratio of women in leadership roles is higher in non-SOEs (e.g. domestic, private, foreign invested). Paradox leadership enables leaders to be more capable of dealing with on-going uncertainty and changes. Western-derived business training on the surge, but insufficient to address daily challenges of business leaders. A self-initiated approach to leader development provides a viable solution to manage tension and conflicts.

Case	Value/thinking and leadership	Western/foreign influence on leadership	Key tensions and concerns of business leaders
Vietnam	Combination of traditional values of Confucianism/Daoism/Buddhism with socialist ideology and market-oriented economic reform. Leadership: paternalism with hierarchy, authoritarianism, benevolence and moral integrity; treating followers as family members (beyond workplace); common goals and self-sacrifice; setting up a role model for others; sufficient knowledge to lead; win-win mindset and social networks; harmony and a mid-way.	French colonial influence; later, Soviet and American influence on management and leadership. Recent increasing MBA- and Western-based education, with graduates' and FOEs' influence on management and leadership: ethical leadership and transformational leadership.	Tensions between conventional Vietnamese leadership styles and practices and adopting and modifying Western concepts/practices in local firms and FOEs. FOEs adopting localization practices and modifying their best practices in local operation. New-generation employees' demand for changing leadership style. Women's leadership participation is relatively high. Leadership competency development is crucial for future success. Successful leaders must have a holistic, contradictory and interrelated view of the world.

political, economic, social and cultural engagement with the West. For example, Singapore, one of the important colonial ports of the British Empire in the past, has maintained many legacies of the British 'rulers', including the judicial system, contractual and transactional underpinnings of economic exchange activities. Business education is also Western-based (i.e. MBAs), predominately under the influence of the US and UK higher education systems. In addition, Singapore has been an important regional headquarters of many MNCs from the West. These companies have brought their management systems and leadership styles into local business operations, in turn exerting a significant impact on leadership in Singapore.

In comparison, Japan, Korea and Taiwan can be seen as another group with strong indigenous management and leadership practices, evolving however, against a backdrop of two-way communication with the West. On the one hand, the US continues to exert substantial influence due to its political, military and economic involvement in the region during the post-WWII period. On the other hand, these economies are more proactive in opening up to foreign investment whereby increasing numbers of local companies are now taking initiatives to internationalize. The two-way economic and business engagement between foreign and local companies has subsequently blurred the boundary of the concepts and practices of management systems and leadership styles. In addition, younger generations of business leaders are now more likely to obtain a Western-style business/management education during their undergraduate and postgraduate studies. Therefore, although the traditional ways of managing and leading business still exist to a certain extent, new ways have been gradually introduced and increasingly hold a significant position.

Our last sample group includes the two socialist market economies of China and Vietnam. These two countries have certain common historical roots politically, socially and culturally. Both were partially (China) or fully (Vietnam) colonized by Western powers, and their so-called modern business/management systems were profoundly influenced by the West during the early 20th Century. However, the subsequent communist revolutionary movements focused on anti-feudalism (including the old ruling class and traditional thinking), anti-imperialism (mainly Western powers and Japanese invasion) and anti-capitalism (mainly market economy with private ownership). As socialist societies, both countries heavily relied on the Soviet Union's systems in the development of their own planning systems and business/management operations. Later, China adopted economic reform and an 'open door' policy, which had an impact on Vietnam, influencing it to change its economic system through *doi moi* (economic renovation). One of the key reform agendas was to improve efficiency and productivity among different ownership companies.

Since then, foreign influence, predominately from the West, has become stronger under the market economic reforms coupled with opening up for international trade and investment. These economic reforms have further generated the introduction of Western influences in other realms of society. Specifically, economic rationalism with strong transaction orientation has had a profound influence on decision-makers, including both government leaders and business leaders. For instance, in recent years the way major universities have offered MBA programmes (e.g. with curriculums, textbooks) for leader development is based mainly on a Western approach. An increasing number of students go overseas (mainly to Western countries) to obtain their undergraduate and postgraduate degrees and then return to their home countries to work. Increasingly, government leaders and business leaders also undertake short-term training programmes overseas (again, mainly in Western countries) to upgrade their leadership competencies. Altogether, these transformations have resulted in mixed leadership styles with elements of traditional, socialist and Western practices (predominately free market and transactional oriented).

Today the key Western concepts of leadership have a profound influence in East Asia. Generally speaking, transactional-oriented economic rationale underlies decision-making in the West and lays the foundation of Western leadership (Zehnder et al., 2017). East Asia is based on systems of social order through hierarchical relationships, which may not be able to deliver effective economic results. Nowadays, all the economies in East Asia are facing increasing competition not only in the region but also globally. The economic survival of any company is the first priority and, therefore, economic rationalism and transactional leadership could be seen as the most influential concepts among business leaders, in particular younger-generation leaders.

Some indigenous leadership practices share common ground with Western leadership concepts that focus on longer-term, relational and collective approaches such as transformational leadership, authentic leadership, ethical leadership and transpersonal leadership (Lord et al., 2016). These leadership forms represent a natural engagement of Eastern and Western concepts in which mutual learning and understanding are the key characteristics. In other words, the emerging Western leadership concepts are starting to incorporate Eastern thinking. One such example of a new leadership concept, namely paradoxical leadership, has made its debut in the Western literature but was developed by Chinese scholars using research methodology derived from the West (Zhang et al., 2015).

The above discussions lead us to consider the third key question: What are the key concerns of business leaders in East Asia in confronting challenges and becoming successful and sustainable leaders?

Business leaders in the six economies studied have raised some important issues (see Table 9.1). First, many business leaders maintained that there is a need to adopt a more balanced approach between established indigenous practices and Western practices under the process of business internationalization. The education system, including MBA courses, should not just teach Western thinking and practices, but should combine these with indigenous approaches. Given that certain Western concepts are learnt from Eastern thinking, building effective and sustainable leadership depends on combining useful Western and Eastern concepts, and mixing leadership styles.

Second, women's leadership is a challenging issue. Though some case study economies might have indicated a better situation (i.e. China and Vietnam) than others (e.g. Japan and Korea), the overall situation points to a lack of women's leadership in business. There is a need for institutional reform and changing organizational cultures in order to encourage and promote women to business leadership positions – this is a fundamental issue for social progress in East Asia.

Third, given the changing economic situation, younger-generation leaders expect to have more tolerance of failure in new economic sectors. Many young graduates with entrepreneurship spirit become involved in start-up businesses, but the success rate has not been high so far. In order for this younger generation to be more risk-taking and innovative, others – including mentors, investors, friends and relatives – need to be more supportive of newly established start-ups and tolerant of failure (Sardana and Zhu, 2017).

Fourth, there is a call for developing a new company culture by combining positive aspects of both old and new elements, such as:

- more opportunities for young employees to participate in decision-making processes;
- treating employees as agents of changes;
- pragmatic evolution with constant adjustment;
- changing the governance system from 'rule of man' to 'rule of law'; transforming the norm of personal virtue with diligence to organizational-based ethical conduct and behaviour;
- more open communication; and
- fair treatment of employees in order to avoid negative nepotism.

Fifth, given the ongoing changes in information and technology, business leader development is crucial for sustainable leadership, and such development should focus to a greater extent on individual performance and competence by linking training, promotion and career development. A leader ought to have the ability to provide a vision that emphasizes reciprocity and meets the need of social transformation. Business leaders also need to have global mindsets, especially in engaging with overseas operations at the higher end of the value chain. Stronger entrepreneurial spirit is required for new business leaders searching for inspirational role models with the capability of navigating towards further reform and transformation.

Comparative analysis of business leaders and leadership in East Asia

In the previous chapters, we responded to the key research questions with examples taken from the six case study economies. By addressing these issues, we observed some similar but also different patterns, which we summarize in Table 9.1 and elaborate in more detail below.

Regarding paternalistic leadership, the six case study economies show different orientations towards authoritarianism. For example, Japanese and Korean leadership styles can be seen as more hierarchical and authoritarian. Neither society has experienced a bottom-up revolution, and the traditional ruling class still dominates. Japanese work relations emphasize horizontal but not vertical harmony; hence, leaders harshly criticize subordinates who make mistakes. Although Korean work relations emphasize both horizontal and vertical harmony, many business leaders obtained their initial leadership training in a military environment that is hierarchical in nature (i.e. compulsory national service). In addition, the traditional feudal system, with a ruling elite class, makes prevalent hierarchical and less respectful attitudes of leaders towards subordinates.

Singapore and Taiwan can be seen as less authoritarian compared with Japan and Korea. Given the strong Western influence in Singapore (i.e. relatively less hieratical) – as well as the Chinese concept of 'company is family', kindness towards subordinates and paternalistic leadership – it can be considered to represent a relative balance between authoritarian and benevolent behaviour. Taiwan's society appears to preserve traditional values to a greater extent than Mainland China in certain respects, due to the latter's 'Cultural Revolution' experience (i.e. destroying the old cultures). Evidence indicates that social harmony and leadership with kindness are crucial for business survival. Many examples of family-owned SMEs show that the owner behaves like a father figure to the business and looks after everyone within the firm. Even nowadays, younger leaders adopt some of these practices and treat their fellow employees as close friends or family members in the workplace. By doing so, when a business faces difficulties, everyone is expected to be responsible for the survival of the business, not just the boss.

The third group of socialist market economies, namely China and Vietnam, are more complex in terms of leadership practices. Both societies were under the strong influence of Confucianism, but experienced a communist-led revolution. Under the socialist planning system, both countries followed the Soviet model. The principle of this model in the field of management was that a manager/leader takes full responsibility by virtue of having power while practising egalitarian treatment of everyone. The principle of equality and fair treatment of employees constrained leaders in the misuse of power. Therefore, even after economic reform when the leadership demonstrated a more transactional-oriented style, business leaders in general, and those who led the public sector, such as SOEs, in particular, combined an authoritarian leadership style with kindness, fairness and virtuous behaviour. This hybrid model of leadership is expected at both upper and lower levels of hierarchy. At the upper levels, the selection criteria for leadership positions need to reflect the aforementioned qualities in addition to knowledge and skills traditionally associated with being a leader. At the lower levels, subordinates would be given an opportunity to comment on the leadership qualities before promotion of a particular leader through a 360-degree survey (feedback), especially in the public sector.

Therefore, from these comparisons we can see that even among East Asian economies there are different types of paternalistic leadership styles: some lean to a greater extent towards authoritarian orientation; others are less authoritarian but more balanced, with benevolent, transformational and authentic elements in forming their leadership style. However, we realize these comparisons are very general and based on national boundaries. The reality of individual cases may be more heterogonous given the personality of individual leaders, their past experience as leader and follower, their training and educational background and so on. These individual backgrounds may impact strongly on leaders' different behaviour beyond national-based generalizations.

Comparative analysis of business leaders and leadership in the East and the West

Another key purpose of this book is to compare some fundamental differences regarding business leaders and leadership in the East and the West based on the illustration of underpinning theories and thinking, as well as on the findings identified in the case study chapters. Table 9.2 summarizes a number of key issues in terms of different reasons, characteristics and ongoing changes.

According to traditional Eastern thinking (i.e. Confucianism), the principal reason for having leaders and leadership is to maintain social order, whether it be within a family where there is a need for a father to lead and guide, a community where there is a need for a chief to lead and coordinate, or even a society where there is a need for a ruler to lead and control the social order (Zhu and Warner, 2004). In contrast, the Western rationale of the need for leaders and leadership is rooted in the economic reason of adequately and efficiently allocating economic resources (Zehnder et al., 2016).

Hence, the Eastern thinking of effective leadership requires absolute authority within a social hierarchy, namely paternalistic and authoritarian leadership, to rule and control subordinates – but ideally with benevolent behaviour. The leadership process focuses on effective and dependent relationships with a group orientation and a balanced way for the purpose of maintaining harmony. Social relationships – or *guanxi*, to use the Chinese term – play an important role in this process (Burt and Burzynaska, 2017). In contrast, Western thinking of effective leadership requires the right leader to be selected with sound economic rationalistic decision-making powers. The leadership process mainly focuses on rational economic resources allocation with transactional-oriented and result-driven behaviour (Zehnder et al., 2016). The interaction between leaders and subordinates is oriented towards the individual and factor-determined interaction, rather than affective and social relationships.

Table 9.2 Comparison of key issues of business leaders and leadership between East and West

East	West
Maintaining social order as initial needs for leaders and leadership	Achieving economic rational outcome as initial needs for leaders and leadership
More focus on power control with authoritarian style	More focus on economic control over resources allocation
Paternalistic leadership style with social hierarchy as fundamental leadership practices	Transactional leadership style with economic rationalism as fundamental leadership practices
Relational-based process with group orientation and a balanced way to maintain harmony (i.e. face culture)	Result-driven process with individual orientation and factor-determined interaction
Increasing modification by adding virtual/benevolence, vision, transformational, situational and authentic leadership behaviours	Increasing modification by adopting more transformational, ethical, authentic and transpersonal leadership behaviours
More fluid and elastic, ready to be adaptable	More clearly defined
Moral obligation toward subordinates is important	Business/economic results are more important

However, our study has observed a mutual learning process between East and West regarding the concepts and practices of leadership, resulting in the emergence of some common ground in recent years (Zhu et al., 2007). On the one hand, Eastern leadership thinking and practices have been influenced by economic rationalism due to globalization of business and management. Transactional-oriented leadership style has had a profound influence in East Asia, and this has been reflected in our case study chapters. Increasing efforts are being made in the modification of the traditional paternalistic leadership style by extending some good elements that are consistent with certain concepts of newly developed Western leadership styles, such as transformational, situational, ethical and authentic leadership. On the other hand, the concepts of leadership in the West have been undergoing a process of rethinking and reforming by linking their economic rationalist underpinning (focused on transactional leadership) with Eastern philosophical concepts (such as a relational-based, collective-oriented vision, with a drive to achieve better human value beyond purely economic bottom lines. This mutual learning and reforming process is ongoing and eventually could lead to a more meaningful development of new concepts and practices of leadership in the future.

Concluding remarks

Based on our illustrations in earlier chapters and the discussion within this chapter, it is clear that one important outcome of a comparative analysis is the realization that the region does not have a single Asian model explaining how to do business and lead business operations and the workforce effectively. The six Asian economies indicate certain similar characteristics, but are also dissimilar due to different paths of development in economic, social, political and cultural realms. This heterogeneity once again establishes the importance of contextual contingencies at various levels (e.g. state, industry, organization) to managerial cognition and action. The implicit expectations of how a business leader looks and behaves are not always consistent with stereotypical Western leader-like traits and behaviours. The complexity is further exacerbated by the expansion of Western-derived best practices and management philosophies which often encounter resistance or challenges from indigenous ways of thinking and of doing, making partial adoption and continuous modification the reality.

To sum up, as we discussed at the beginning of the book, a major challenge for advancing research and the practices of business leaders and leadership lies in the acquisition of the right competencies and the process of selecting leaders with such competencies. Underpinning theories and fundamental concepts present 'idealist' models of leaders and leadership, but the reality is far more complex than these approaches. Leaders with poor ideas and poor behaviour are to be found at every level nowadays – at national, community and organizational levels. Teaching and learning to be a good leader is one thing, but implementing these factors in practice is another, particularly when leaders are confronted with economic pressure or crises in their lives. Further research may focus to a greater extent on how to select the right leaders, how to deal with negative leaders (i.e. prevention or elimination), and how to make leaders and leadership sustainable. By compiling this book, we hope to have contributed greater dialogue and debate between the Eastern and Western ways of thinking and acting regarding business leaders and leadership, and to have enhanced the future development of leadership globally.

References

Burt, R.S. and Burzynaska, K. (2017) 'Chinese entrepreneurs, social networks, and guanxi', *Management and Organizational Review*, 13(2): 221–260.

Lord, R.G., Gatti, P. and Chui, S.L.M. (2016) 'Social-cognitive, relational, and identity-and based approaches to leadership', *Organizational Behavior and Human Decision Processes*, 136: 119–134.

Rindova, V.P. and Starbuck, W.H. (1997) 'Ancient Chinese theories of control', *Journal of Management Inquiry*, 6(2): 144–159.

Sardana, D. and Zhu, Y. (2017) *Conducting Business in China and India: A Comparative and Contextual Analysis*, London and New York: Palgrave Macmillan.

Watson, B. (1964) *Han Fei Tzu: Basic Writings*, New York: Columbia University Press.

Zehnder, C., Herz, H. and Bonardi, J.P. (2017) 'A productive clash of cultures: Injecting economics into leadership research', *Leadership Quarterly*, 28(1): 65–85.

Zhang, Y., Waldman, D.A., Han, Y.L. and Li, X.B. (2015) 'Paradoxical leader behaviors in people management: Antecedents and consequences', *Academy of Management Journal*, 58(2): 538–566.

Zhu, Y. and Warner, M. (2004) 'HRM in East Asia', in A. W. Harzing and J. V. Ruysseveldt (eds), *International Human Resource Management* (2nd edition), London: Sage, pp. 195–220.

Zhu, Y., Warner, M. and Rowley, C. (2007) 'Human resource management with Asian characteristics: A hybrid people management system in East Asia', *International Journal of Human Resource Management*, 18: 44–67.

Index